William Dressler

Peters' Catholic Class Book

William Dressler

Peters' Catholic Class Book

ISBN/EAN: 9783337376246

Printed in Europe, USA, Canada, Australia, Japan

Cover: Foto ©Thomas Meinert / pixelio.de

More available books at **www.hansebooks.com**

PETERS'
CATHOLIC CLASS BOOK;

A COLLECTION OF COPYRIGHT

Songs, Duets, Trios, and Choruses,

SUITABLE FOR

JUVENILE CLASSES, CONVENTS, SEMINARIES, AND THE HOME CIRCLE.

INCLUDING

AN EASY, CONCISE AND SYSTEMATIC COURSE OF ELEMENTARY INSTRUCTION, WITH ATTRACTIVE EXERCISES.

THE WHOLE COMPILED AND ARRANGED

BY

WILLIAM DRESSLER.

Published by J. L. PETERS, 599 Broadway, New York.

St. Louis,	Cincinnati,	Detroit,	Boston,
T. A. BOYLE.	DOBMEYER & CODY.	C. J. WHITNEY & CO.	P. DONAHOE.

Entered according to Act of Congress, in the year 1872, by J. L. PETERS, in the Office of the Librarian of Congress, at Washington.

PREFACE.

"PETERS' CATHOLIC CLASS BOOK" has been prepared expressly to suit the wants of the Religious Orders, and others engaged in Catholic Class Teaching, and is presented in the belief that it will supply a long-felt want, viz.: a *Secular* Vocal Class Book, *containing Catholic Hymns, instead of Protestant Tunes.*

Vocal music has now a recognized place in the list of studies in nearly every public school in the United States; and as parents are insisting on having their children taught Music, it becomes a matter of necessity that our Catholic schools should follow in the same track. This has already been done by many of our larger schools, and the others would have done so, but for the lack of a suitable CLASS BOOK—they rightly objecting to the introduction of books containing objectionable Protestant tunes, such as all the public school singing books are filled with. "PETERS' CATHOLIC CLASS BOOK" has been prepared expressly to fill this want, and it is for this reason that we have introduced both Sacred and Secular Songs—hoping thereby, to cause its general adoption as a Vocal Class Book in the numerous Catholic schools of the United States and Canadas; thus giving an opportunity to the Catholic children—of both rich and poor—to acquire a knowledge of music, and early familiarizing themselves with *pronounced* Catholic Hymns.

In compiling the work, the Author has followed our instructions, "*to select only the best material,*" and with this view he has given the preference to the Elementary matter contained in THE SONG ECHO, a well-known school book by H. S. Perkins. The Secular Songs have been selected from the works of our most popular song writers, and with special regard to the moral character of the words. The Catholic Hymns are mainly selected from the "May Blossoms," and "Peters' Sodality Hymn Book," both works by the Sisters of Notre Dame, Cincinnati, Ohio; which, with the numerous choice arrangements of Mr. Dressler, completes a work, that we are confident will tend to elevate and spiritualize the youthful heart and mind, when assembled at their little exercises, Sodality devotions, etc., and to give to *study* itself an attraction which will divest it, of much of the labor which renders *study* so distasteful to most children.

THE PUBLISHER.

PETERS' CATHOLIC CLASS BOOK.

A COLLECTION OF SACRED AND SECULAR MUSIC.
ARRANGED FOR JUVENILE CLASSES by WM. DRESSLER.

Price, 75 cents each; $7.50 per dozen.

CONTENTS.

CLASSIFICATION.

PART I.—ELEMENTARY INSTRUCTIONS..Pages 5-35
Chapter I.—Practice and Theory.......... 5
" II.—Staff and Notes.............. 6
" III.—Letters, Clefs, and Pitch...... 8
" IV.—Scales and Intervals Illust'd.. 11
" V.—Notes, Rest, and Measures.... 15
" VI.—Expression.................. 23
" VII.—Chromatic Intervals and Scale 25
" VIII.—Minor Scale................. 27
" IX.—Transposition................ 32

Chapter X.—Major and Minor Scale........ 32
PART II.—EXERCISES, ROUNDS, ETC....... 36-38
PART III.—MISCELLANEOUS SONGS, ETC... 39-70
    SCHOOL SONGS, ETC............. 77-100
    MORAL AND INSTRUCTIVE 101-113
PART IV—RELIGIOUS, SACRED, AND DE-
    VOTIONAL SONGS; HYMNS TO
    THE BLESSED VIRGIN, MAY
    HYMNS; HYMNS IN HONOR OF
    SAINTS........................114-256

ALPHABETICAL INDEX.

	Page.
Acts of Faith, Desire, and Spiritual Communion. 2 or 4 voices......*Peters' Sodality H. B.*	181
Act of Contrition. 2 or 4 v....*Crown of Jesus.*	172
Adeste fideles, No. 1. O come, all ye faithful (Christmas H'n). 2 or 4 v. mix....*Portuguese.*	154
Adeste fideles, No. 2. O come, all ye faithful Christmas Hymn......*Peters' Sodality H. B.*	156
Advent Hymn (Come, O divine Messiah)........	150
Advent Hymn (Creator alme siderum).........	151
Again we meet (Commencement Hymn). 2-pt. Cho.................................*Dressler.*	77
Again this holy morn. Dt. or Qt.....*Hays.*	156
Ah! must I leave (Farewell to May). *F. Songs.*	240
Ah! ye that in the cloister dwell (Hymn to St. Scholastica). 3-pt. Cho. and Soli....*Dressler.*	254
And thou art no more (Death of a Schoolmate).	99
Angel voices. Dt. and Cho. *ad lib*....*Shattuck.*	50
Annunciation Hymn (How pure)......*S. N. D.*	199
As onward thro' this vale (Fear not but trust in Providence). Song ....*Persley.*	120
Assumption Hymn. Trio......*Lambillotte.*	224
As the gentle spring (Mary, Mother sweet). Dt. and 2-pt. Cho....................*Concone.*	232
Ave Sanctissima (Evening Song to the Virgin). Duet.............................*Hemans.*	140
Ave Maria, bright and pure. Dt......*S. N. D.*	205
Ave Maria Stella ....*S. N. D.*	198
Beautiful flowers for my mother......*Higgins.*	46
Blessed Sacrament (Jesus, my God). Solo and 2-pt. Cho....................*May Blossoms.*	182
By the first bright Easter day ...*Mendelssohn.*	171
Charity (Meek and lowly)..............*Glover.*	110
Chaplet of ros's (A child of thine). Dt.*Jamissial.*	194
Christian soul (Yoke of Christ). 2 or 4 v.,*Pleyel.*	129
Christmas songs............Pp. 152, 153, 154,	156
Come, oh! divine Messiah (Advent Hymn). Dt. or 2-pt. Cho....................*Lambillotte.*	150
Come, Creator Spirit.....*Peters' Sodality H. B.*	174
Commencement Hymn. 2-pt. Cho...*Dressler.*	77
Confirmation Hymn. *Peters' Catholic Melodist.*	185
Consolation (Tho' sorrow may darken). *Long.*	102
Coronation Song (These crowns for you). Song for Dt. and 3-pt. Cho..........*W. C. Peters.*	90
Creator alme siderum (Vesper Hymn for the Sundays in Advent).............*Gregorian.*	151
Cross and Crown. Duet and Cho....*Thomas.*	122

	Page.
Drifting with the tide. Duet.........*Kinkel.*	101
Don't be sorrowful, darling...........*Webster.*	104
Do right and fear not. Duet and Cho. *Thomas.*	116
Desire of Heaven ......*Peters' Sodality H. B.*	128
Dear little one! (Hymn to the Infant Jesus). Dt. and 2-pt. Cho. or Quart................*Hays.*	159
Dear angel, ever at my side (Hymn to my guardian angel). Dt. or Qt.*Peters' Sodality H. B.*	243
Eve of Communion ....*Lambillotte.*	180
Evening Song to the Virgin..........*Hemans.*	140
Evening closes (Vesper Hymn to the Virgin). Solo, Duet, and 4-pt. Fem. Cho..*W. C. Peters.*	192
Eve of May. Dt. or Ch. and Solo..*Lambillotte.*	230
Easter Songs...................Pp. 170 and	171
Evening Song............See pp. 187, 189, 190,	192
Fear not, but trust in Providence .....*Persley.*	120
Father, hear us. Duet, Solo, and Cho.*Thomas.*	136
Father, ever keep me near thee........*Persley.*	138
Four great truths. 2 or 4 v............*Hemy.*	177
Fold we our hands (Evening Song)..*Buildieu.*	187
Fading, still fading..............*Wiesenthal.*	189
Farewell to May (Ah! must I leave)..*F. Longs.*	240
God bless my boy......................*Bishop.*	55
Greeting. Duet or 2-pt. Cho....*Mendelssohn.*	51
Good night. Trio or 3-pt. Cho....*Wyman.*	88
Good-bye, till I see you again. Song....*Hays.*	92
God of Orphans. 2-pt. Cho............*Westlake.*	133
Gently, Lord, oh! gently lead us......*Danks.*	144
God of Might. 2-pt. Cho.,*Peters' Sodality H. B.*	147
Gentle Star of Ocean...............*S. N. D.*	198
Glory to God (Magnificat) .....*Verschneider,*	202
Go ye forth (Hymn for the Religious Profession).	242
Glorious Mysteries (By the first bright Easter day). 2-pt. Cho...............*Mendelssohn.*	171
He wipes the tear. Duet ....*Danks.*	118
Heart of the Holy Child. *Peters' Sodality H. B.*	160
Holy Church, thou art our Mother. 2 or 4 mix. voices........................*Crown of Jesus.*	173
Hail! sweet temperance. 2 or 4 v.....*Hemy.*	179
Holy Communion (O dearest Lord).....*S. N. D.*	153
Hail! Queen of Heaven. *Peters' Sodality H. B.*	196
Hail! Holy Queen. Dt. and 2-pt. Cho...*W. D.*	197
Holy Mary, Mother mild. S. and Cho.*Dressler.*	218
Hail! Virgin, dearest Mary (May Hymn). Cho. and Solo....................*May Blossoms.*	238

CONTENTS.

Title	Composer	Page
Heart of Mary	Peters' Sodality H. B.	219
Hymn for Religious Profession (Go ye forth). S. and 2-pt. Cho.	Weber.	242
Hymn to my guardian angel (Dear Angel. Dt. or Qt.	Peters' Sodality H. B.	245
Hail! Holy Joseph. Dt. and 4-pt. Cho.	Lambillotte.	248
Holy Joseph. Duet and Solo.	Niedermeyer.	247
Holy Name of Jesus (Jesus, the only thought). Solo and 3-pt. Cho.	Peters' Sodality H. B.	161
Hail! Mary. Chant		
How pure, how frail (Annunciation)	S. N. D.	199
Hymn for a Patron Saint (Sweet Saint). Duet.		246
I am happy, mother, darling. Song	Persley.	48
I want to be an angel. Solo and Cho.	Dressler.	79
In the graveyard softly sleeping. Dt.	Martin.	100
If you love me, do my will. Solo.	Thomas.	140
Image [The] of our Queen (This is the image).		234
Immaculate Conception	I'p.	203 and 204
Improve the passing hour. Trio.	Westrop.	39
Judge not, there's pardon for all. Song.	Cos.	114
Jesus, the only thought (Holy Name). Solo and 3-pt. Cho.	Peters' Sodality H. B.	161
Jesus, my God, my all. Dt. or mix. Qt.	Dressler.	163
Jesus and the children (Some dear little children). Dt. or 2-pt. Cho. and Solo	Dressler.	166
Jesus Crucified (O come and mourn). Dt. or mix. Qt.	Peters' Sodality H. B.	169
Jesus Christ is risen (Easter Hymn)	Dressler.	170
Joy of my heart (May Hymn). Trio.	Lambillotte.	235
Jesus, my God (Blessed Sacrament). Solo and 2-pt. Cho.	May Blossoms.	182
Kiss me, good night, mamma. Song	Hays.	50
Lucis Creator (O great Creator). Vesper Hymn for Sundays	Peters' Sodality H. B.	175
Litany of the Blessed Virgin.	Wesley.	200
Little feet so white and fair. Song	Persley.	40
Little voices heard no more. Song	Persley.	42
Little Maud (O yes, she is dainty)	Webster.	44
Little [The] brown church. Song and Cho.	Pitts.	72
Lonely, oh! so lonely. Song	Kinkel.	64
Let us ever be happy. Song	Graff.	82
Let us try to be happy. Song	Laurence.	84
Let us sing merrily. 2-pt. Cho.	Westrop.	83
List to the convent bells. 1 or 2 v.	Blockley.	86
Lord, teach me how to pray. Song.	Wallace.	134
Lover of a little child. Dt. or 2-pt. Cho.	Dressler.	165
Love of Jesus (O come, my sweet Saviour). Dt. or 2-pt. Cho.	Peters' Sodality H. B.	168
My sister in Heaven. Song and Cho.	Gorham.	53
Motherless and fatherless. Song.	Tucker.	70
Memorial flowers. Dt. or Cho.	Mendelssohn.	98
Morning prayer. Dt. or Cho.	Dressler.	188
Magnificat (Glory to God). Cho. & S.	Verschneider.	202
Mater admirabilis (O mater). S. and Cho.	Concone.	206
Memorare. Cho. and Solo.	Lambillotte.	208
Mother of Jesus (Mother, most holy).	Lambillotte.	210
Mother, loved (Mary, hear my fervent prayer). Dt. or 2-pt. Cho. and Solo.	Lambillotte.	212
Maiden Mother. Dt. and 3-pt. Ch.	Crown of Jesus.	214
Mary blest. Dt. or 2-pt. Ch., T. & B. ad lib.	Hemy.	215
Mary, Queen of my soul. S & 2-pt. Ch.	Wollaston.	216
Mary's titles (Thro' the world)	S. N. D.	217
Mary, Mother sweet (As the gentle spring). May Hymn. Dt. and 2-pt. Cho.	Concone.	232
Mary, Queen of all the flowers	Lambillotte.	236
My Angel (O list, my loved Angel)	S. N. D.	244
Mystery of love. Solo and 2-pt. Cho.	S. N. D.	184
My Saviour, as thou wilt. Dt. or Cho.	Frey.	164
My God, accept my heart (Confirmation Hymn). 2-pt. Cho.	Peters' Sodality H. B.	185
No home to shelter. Song	Stanley.	60
Nobody's darling (Out in this cold world)	Hays.	6
Never speak ill of the dead	Justin Juch.	11
O come all ye faithful (Adeste fideles), No. 1. 2 or 4 v.	Portuguese.	18
O come all ye faithful (Adeste fideles), No. 2. or 4 v.	Peters' Sodality H. B.	18
O come and mourn with me (Jesus Crucified). Dt. or mix. Qt.	Peters' Sodality H. B.	16
Oh. no! not sad. Song	Bishop.	
On the death of a schoolmate (And thou art no more). Trio or Cho.	German.	
O Jesus who for love for me. 2 or 4 v.	Beethoven.	
Our Father, Hail Mary. Chant		1
O purest of creatures (Immaculate Conception). Solo and 2-pt. Qt.	Osthoff.	2
Our queen immaculate. Solo and Ch.	Are Maria.	2
Ora pro me. Duet.	S. N. D.	2
Our lady of help. Dt. and Ch.	Lambillotte.	2
O Sanctissima. Dt. or 2-pt. Ch.	Stubelt.	2
O Sanctissima. Dt. or 2-pt. Cho.	Sicilian.	2
O God of Orphans. 2-pt. Cho.	Westlake.	1
Papa, come help me across the dark river. Song and 2-pt. Cho. with T. and B. ad lib.	Persley.	
Papa, stay home. Song	Hays.	
Please, papa, do come home early	Dressler.	
Pray for the dead. 2 or 4 v. mixed	Dressler.	1
Praise the Lord (Laudate dominum). Chant.		
Petitions of Mary. Solo and Cho.	Lambillotte.	2
Patron Saint (Hymn in honor)	Crown of Jesus.	2
Rock of ages. Duet.	Frey.	1
Rule of life. 2-pt. Cho.	Mozart.	1
Rose of the Cross. Duet	May Blossoms.	2
Saints (Hymns in honor of)	Pp.	245-2
See amid the winter's snow (Christmas Hymn).		1
Stabat Mater.	May Blossoms.	2
Safe in the ark (Little one)	Tucker.	
Sweet mother, pray for me	Millard.	
Seek and ye shall find (Oh! weary soul)	Bishop.	1
Speak the truth (When you are guilty).	S. Dressler.	1
Safe at home beyond temptation	Walker.	1
Strike the harp in praise of God	Nelson.	1
Sweet Heart of Jesus	Peters' Sodality H. B.	2
Sweet Lady of the Sacred Heart	S. N. D.	2
Sorrows of Mary	Verschneider.	2
St. Agatha (We come to thee)	Dressler.	2
St. Agnes. Dt. and 3-pt. Cho.	Crown of Jesus.	2
St. Catherine (Sweet St. Catherine)	Hemy.	2
St. Aloysius. Dt. and Ch.	Lambillotte.	2
St. Joseph (Holy Joseph)	Neidermeyer.	2
St. Joseph (Hail! Holy Joseph)	Lambillotte.	2
St. Patrick (Hail! Patron of Erin)	Raphaelson.	2
St. Scholastica. 3-pt. Cho. and Solo.	Dressler.	2
Seven Sacraments	Crown of Jesus.	1
Take me, my Jesus	Peters' Sodality H. B.	2
'Tis sad to part. Song and Qt.	Mortimer.	2
True [The] Cross (No wreath of roses). Duet, Alto Solo and Cho. T. and B. ad lib.	Hemy.	2
To thy temple I repair. S. and Cho. or Qt.	Frey.	2
Ten commandments. 2 or 4 mixed v.	Mozart.	2
Unfold, unfold (The Assumption)	Lambillotte.	2
Veni Creator	Peters' Sodality H. B.	2
Vivat Pastor bonus (Welcome. Song to a Bishop or Pastor). 3-pt. Ch. and Dt.	Dressler.	
Welcome. Song to a Bishop or Pastor (Vivat Pastor bonus). 3-pt. Cho. and Dt.	Dressler.	
Will [The] and the way	Clayton.	1
The will of God (The stars as they glimmer). Solo	Swiss.	1
While shepherds watched their flock	Tomlins.	1
You'll think of me, friends, when I'm gone.		
You could not help but love her. Song.	Adam.	1
Yoke [The] of Christ. 2 or 4 v.	Pleyel.	1

PART I.

ELEMENTARY INSTRUCTION.

CHAPTER I.

PRACTICE AND THEORY.

TO THE TEACHER. In presenting the subject of MUSICAL NOTATION in any of its departments, experience proves that oral instruction, mostly by *example*, should first be given to a pupil, or class of pupils. In elementary instruction, *not* "Theory and Practice," but *Practice and Theory;* that is, never, as a rule, give signs and characters as a symbol, or representative of something, until after the *something* has been produced.

If this method of teaching is kept in mind, and practiced, the necessity of some written character or sign will usually suggest itself to the mind of the pupil, by which means thought and invention—so to speak—will be called out. An active and vigorous exercise of the mind upon the subject under consideration is a very important point to gain.

The few principles under each head, or chapter, should be presented clearly, every definition and explanation short and to the point; very seldom repeating the same idea, or fact, in different language, for by so doing, the pupil often becomes confused, and the point, which otherwise might have been gained, is lost, because of a multiplicity of words.

A TONE is a *musical sound,* produced by the even and uninterrupted vibration of some sonorous or elastic body in the air.

TONE is *breath made vocal;* consequently, the more breath,—other things being equal,—the more tone, or voice.

SINGING consists in a prescribed utterance of tone, combined with a clear and distinct enunciation and pronunciation of syllable and words, and in a consistent rendering of the music—called *expression*.

NOTE. TONE and NOISE are specific terms; the former meaning a *musical* sound, and the latter an *unmusical* sound. SOUND is a general term, applied to either.

FIRST WORK TO BE DONE.

A written exercise is unnecessary for either teacher or pupils. A tone, at any convenient pitch, should first be produced, speaking LA, AH, or any monosyllable, and the class imitate. This method should be followed until all the tones of the scale have been presented and learned, and can be sung by numbers, syllables, &c.

THE SCALE

is a succession of eight tones, arranged in a prescribed order.

DIAGRAM OF THE SCALE.

NAMES OR NUMBERS.	NOTES.	SYLLABLES.
8	𝅘𝅥	Do
7	𝅘𝅥	Si
6	𝅘𝅥	La
5	𝅘𝅥	Sol
4	𝅘𝅥	Fa
3	𝅘𝅥	Mi
2	𝅘𝅥	Re
1	𝅘𝅥	Do

NOTE. The explanation of intervals may be deferred a few lessons.

ELEMENTARY INSTRUCTION.

CHAPTER II.

STAFF AND NOTES.

The staff consists of five parallel lines and the four spaces between the lines, thus:

Each line and space is called a DEGREE, of which there are nine, and counted from the lowest upward.

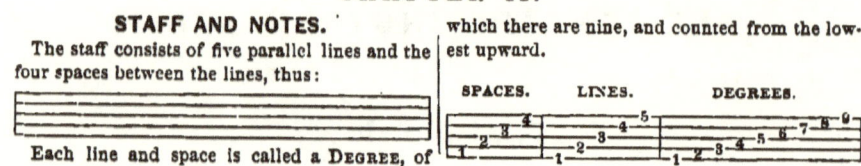

NOTE. The following scale illustrations should be sung.

SCALE UPON THE STAFF.

The above exercise begins upon the first line. Eight degrees are required to represent the scale. Notes are written upon the staff, and represent tones.

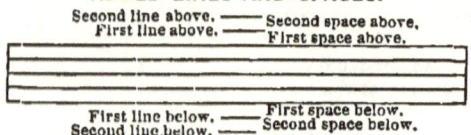

The above scale commences upon the first space.

Notes written upon lower degrees of the staff represent lower tones, and upon higher degrees, higher tones.

ADDED LINES AND SPACES.

When it is necessary to use more than the nine degrees of the staff, lines or spaces may be used, either above or below the staff, as illustrated above.

The above exercise commences upon the second line, or third degree.

ELEMENTARY INSTRUCTION.

The above exercise commences upon the first space below.

The above exercise commences upon the first line below.

EXERCISES FOR PRACTICE.

No. 1. Commencing upon which degree?

1	1	2	2	1	1	2	2	3	3	2	2	1	1	2	3	2
la,	la,	la,	la,	la,	la,	la,	la,	la,	la,	la,	la,	la,	la,	la,	la,	la,
Do,	Do,	Re,	Re,	Do,	Do,	Re,	Re,	Mi,	Mi,	Re,	Re,	Do,	Do,	Re,	Mi,	Re,

1	2	3	4	4	3	3	2	2	1	1	1	2	3	2	1
la,	la,	la,	la,	la,	la,	la,	la,	la,	la,	la,	la,	la	la,	la,	la.
Do,	Re,	Mi,	Fa,	Fa,	Mi,	Mi,	Re,	Re,	Do,	Do,	Do,	Re,	Mi,	Re,	Do.

No. 2. Commencing upon which degree?

1	1	2	2	1	1	2	2	3	3	2	2	1	1	2	2	3
Do,	Do,	Re,	Re,	Do,	Do,	Re,	Re,	Mi,	Mi,	Re,	Re,	Do,	Do,	Re,	Re,	Mi,

3	4	4	3	2	1	2	3	4	5	5	5	4	3	2	1
Mi,	Fa,	Fa,	Mi,	Re,	Do,	Re,	Mi,	Fa,	Sol,	Sol,	Sol,	Fa,	Mi,	Re,	Do.

No. 3. Commencing upon which degree?

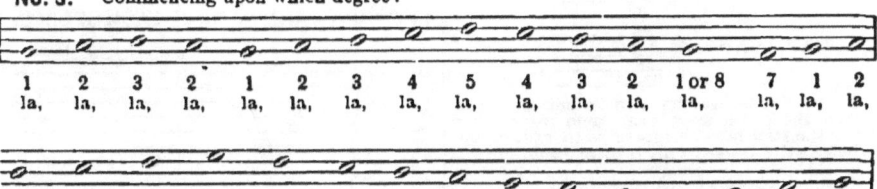

1	2	3	2	1	2	3	4	5	4	3	2	1 or 8	7	1	2
la,	la,	la,	la,	la,	la,	la,	la,	la,	la,	la,	la,	la,	la,	la,	la,

3	4	5	6	5	4	3	2	1	7	6	5	6	7	1 or 8
la,	la,	la,	la,	la,	la,	la,	la,	la	la,	la,	la	la,	la,	la.

No. 4. Commencing where?

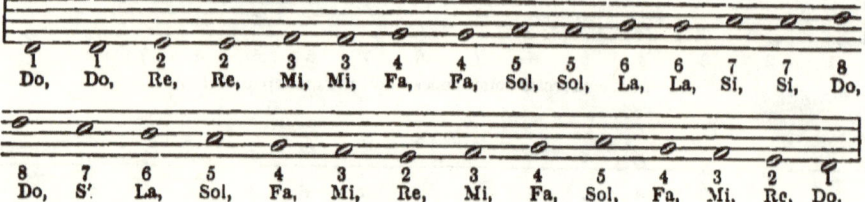

No. 5. Commencing upon which degree?

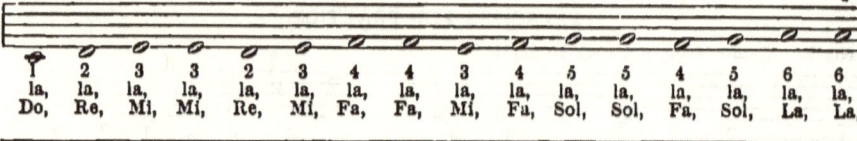

We may commence to write the scale or an exercise upon any degree of the staff, unless a sign is used to indicate otherwise, which will be understood after advancing further with the lessons.

NOTE. Although the syllables which are commonly sung and associated with the tones of the scale usually accompany the exercises through the elementary course, yet it is advised to make but little use of them. To sing with LA, or some other monosyllable, is preferred, as surer progress will be made in reading by exercising the mind upon INTERVALS, rather than by associating the tone with some syllable.

CHAPTER III.

LETTERS, CLEFS, ABSOLUTE PITCH.

The first seven letters of the alphabet, A, B, C, D, E, F, G, are used in music. The character used to determine the (letter) name of each degree is called a Clef, viz:

The G, or Treble clef

The F, or Base clef.

NOTE. These are the two in common use. When the clef is used, each tone represented upon the staff has absolute or *positive* pitch; but when no clef is used, only *relative* pitch.

The Tenor clef is also used.

THE G CLEF AND NAME OF EACH DEGREE.

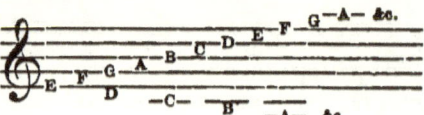

THE F CLEF AND NAME OF EACH DEGREE.

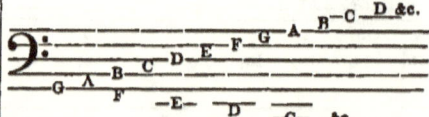

NOTE. It will be observed that, in ascending, the letters occur in alphabetic order; and in descending, the inversion of that order.

ELEMENTARY INSTRUCTION.

THE SCALE UPON THE STAFF, WITH THE G CLEF.

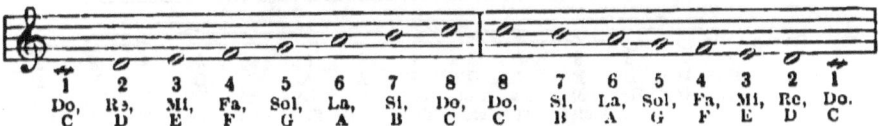

THE SCALE, WITH THE F CLEF.

NOTE. By common consent, the scale is represented upon the staff when the two clefs are used, as in the above examples. It will be observed that C is the starting-point, or ONE; hence the scale is said to be in the KEY OF C.

EXERCISES FOR SPECIAL PRACTICE.

No. 6. Sing by name, letter, syllable, and la.

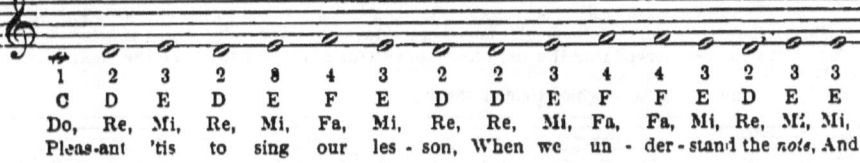

No. 7. Commencing with which tone of the scale?

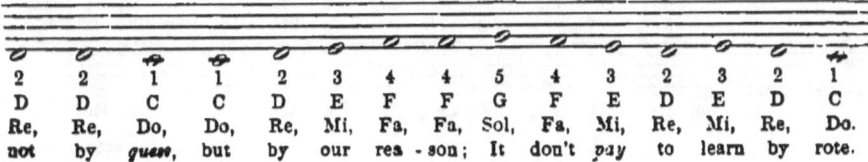

ELEMENTARY INSTRUCTION.

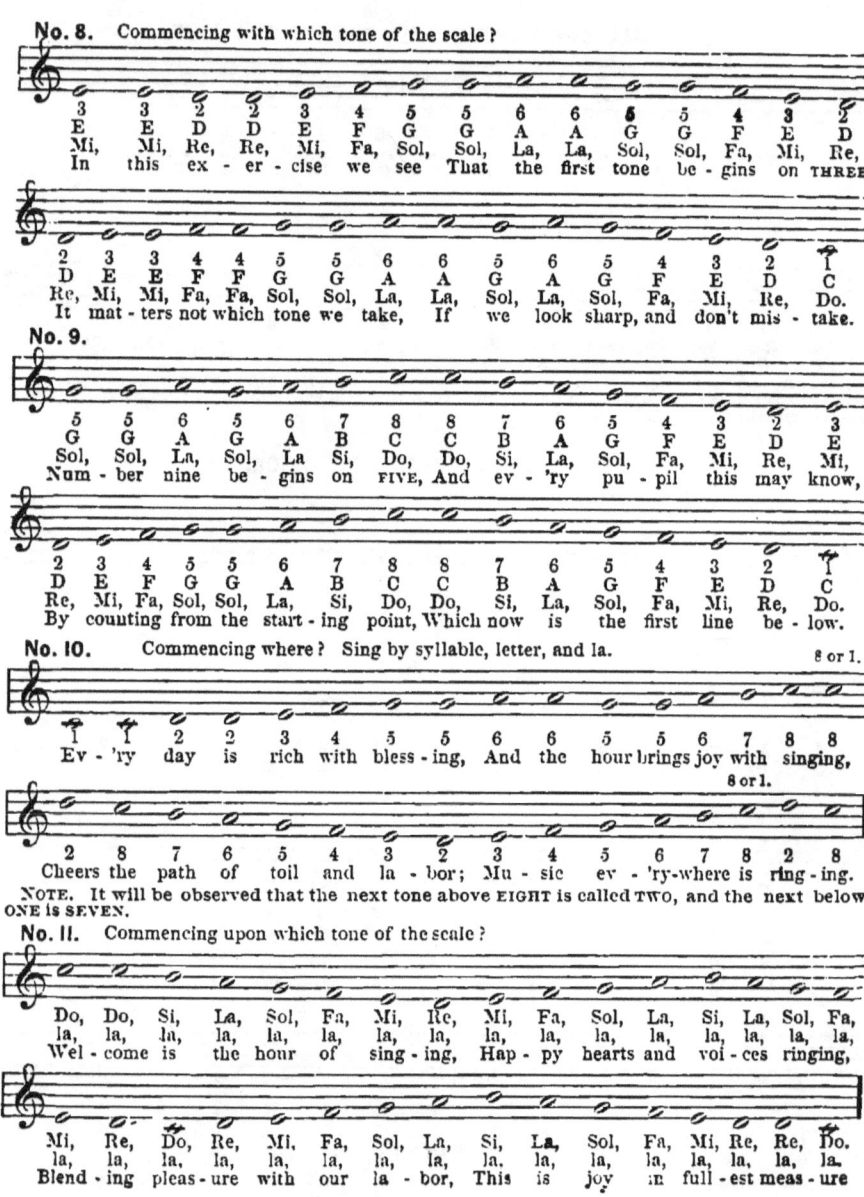

ELEMENTARY INSTRUCTION. 11

CHAPTER IV.
INTERVALS.

The difference in pitch between any two tones is called an interval.

The name *Second* is given to the interval between any two consecutive tones of the scale, as from 1 to 2; 2 to 3; 5 to 6, &c.

There are two kinds of Seconds in the Scale,—large and small, as will be observed.

The large Second is called MAJOR, (meaning *greater*), and the small Second, MINOR, (meaning *less*.)

THE SCALE AND INTERVALS ILLUSTRATED.

```
8 . . . . . . . . . . 𝄽 . . . . . . . Do
         A minor second.
7 . . . . . . . . . . 𝄽 . . . . . . . Si
         A major second.
6 . . . . . . . . . . 𝄽 . . . . . . . La
         A major second.
5 . . . . . . . . . . 𝄽 . . . . . . . Sol
         A major second.
4 . . . . . . . . . . 𝄽 . . . . . . . Fa
         A minor second.
3 . . . . . . . . . . 𝄽 . . . . . . . Mi
         A major Second.
2 . . . . . . . . . . 𝄽 . . . . . . . Re
         A major second.
1 . . . . . . . . . . 𝄽 . . . . . . . Do
```

SCALE INTERVALS (SECONDS) REPRESENTED UPON THE STAFF.

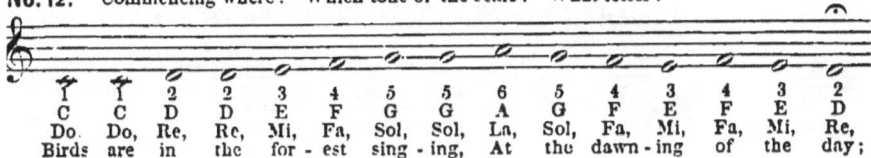

EXERCISES FOR PRACTICE, CONTINUED.

NOTE. When the *Hold* (𝄐) is used the tone may be prolonged.

No. 12. Commencing where? Which tone of the scale? What letter?

ELEMENTARY INSTRUCTION.

No. 13. Commencing where? Which tone of the scale?

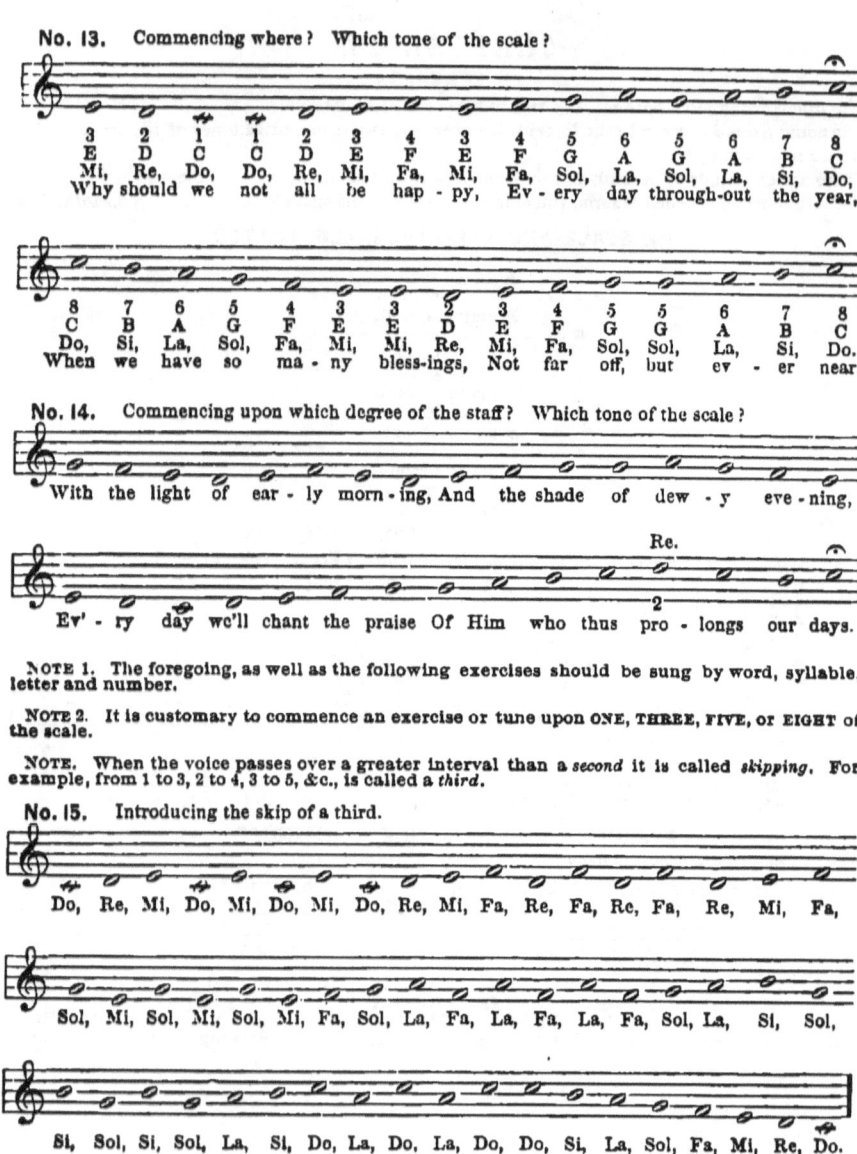

3	2	1	1	2	3	4	3	4	5	6	5	6	7	8
E	D	C	C	D	E	F	E	F	G	A	G	A	B	C
Mi,	Re,	Do,	Do,	Re,	Mi,	Fa,	Mi,	Fa,	Sol,	La,	Sol,	La,	Si,	Do,
Why	should	we	not	all	be	hap	- py,	Ev	- ery	day	through-out	the	year,

8	7	6	5	4	3	3	2	3	4	5	5	6	7	8
C	B	A	G	F	E	E	D	E	F	G	G	A	B	C
Do,	Si,	La,	Sol,	Fa,	Mi,	Mi,	Re,	Mi,	Fa,	Sol,	Sol,	La,	Si,	Do.
When	we	have	so	ma	- ny	bless-ings,	Not	far	off,	but	ev	- er	near.

No. 14. Commencing upon which degree of the staff? Which tone of the scale?

With the light of ear - ly morn - ing, And the shade of dew - y eve - ning,

Re.

Ev' - ry day we'll chant the praise Of Him who thus pro - longs our days.

NOTE 1. The foregoing, as well as the following exercises should be sung by word, syllable, letter and number.

NOTE 2. It is customary to commence an exercise or tune upon ONE, THREE, FIVE, or EIGHT of the scale.

NOTE. When the voice passes over a greater interval than a *second* it is called *skipping*. For example, from 1 to 3, 2 to 4, 3 to 5, &c., is called a *third*.

No. 15. Introducing the skip of a third.

Do, Re, Mi, Do, Mi, Do, Mi, Do, Re, Mi, Fa, Re, Fa, Re, Fa, Re, Mi, Fa,

Sol, Mi, Sol, Mi, Sol, Mi, Fa, Sol, La, Fa, La, Fa, La, Fa, Sol, La, Si, Sol,

Si, Sol, Si, Sol, La, Si, Do, La, Do, La, Do, Do, Si, La, Sol, Fa, Mi, Re, Do.

ELEMENTARY INSTRUCTION.

13

ELEMENTARY INSTRUCTION.

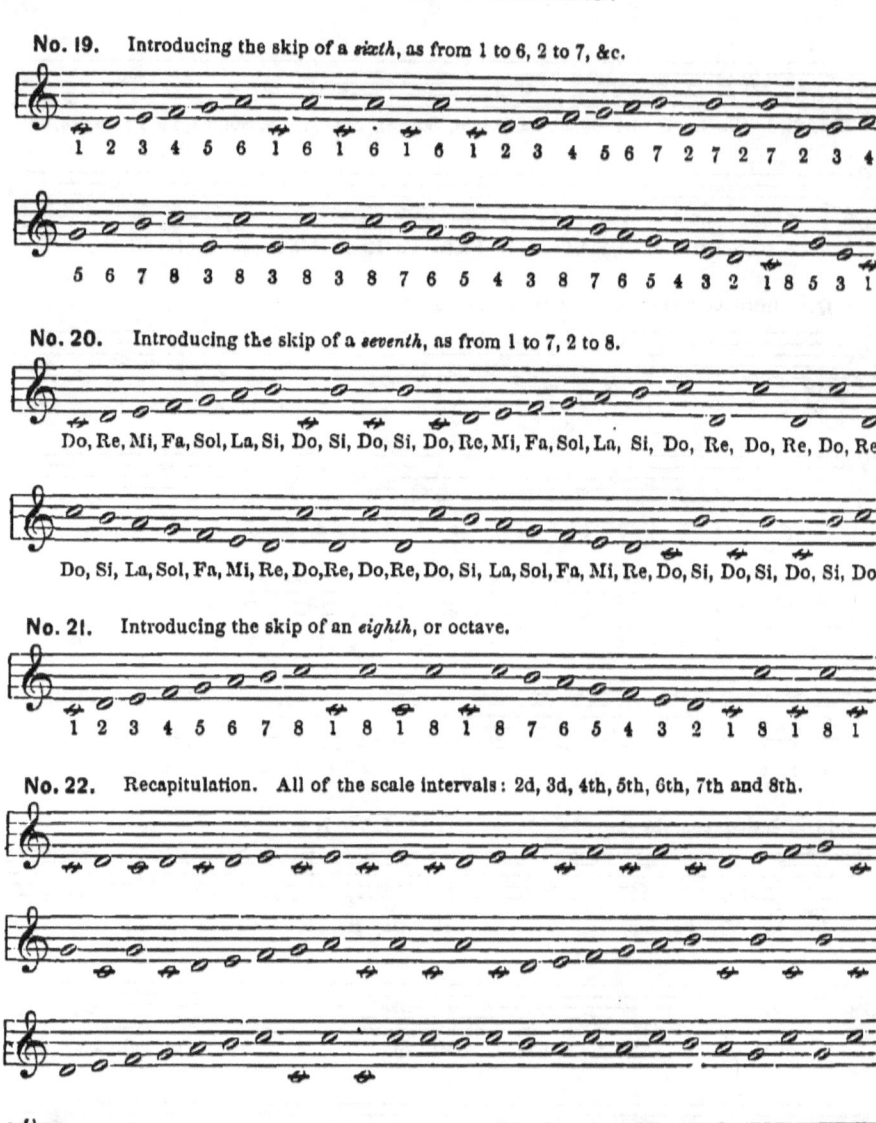

CHAPTER V.

NOTES, RESTS AND MEASURES.

Diagram of Notes and Rests.

The whole note is written thus:— 𝅝	The whole rest is written thus:— ▬
The half note 𝅗𝅥	The half rest ▬
The quarter note ♩	The quarter rest 𝄽
The eighth note ♪	The eighth rest 𝄾
The sixteenth note ♬	The sixteenth rest 𝄿
The thirty-second note	The thirty-second rest

NOTES represent tones, and *rests* indicate silence; but they have no positive value, only relative. For example, a whole note (𝅝) is equal in value to two half notes (𝅗𝅥 𝅗𝅥), or four quarters (♩ ♩ ♩ ♩), &c.

Measures are indicated upon the staff by vertical lines, called bars.

MEASURE. BAR. MEASURE. BAR. MEASURE. BAR. MEASURE. DOUBLE BAR.

NOTE. A double bar is usually placed at the end of a piece of music, and a large bar at the end of a line.

ACCENT.

Measure is a rhythmical division of the music, and consequently indicates the accent.
The most simple kind of measure is called DOUBLE, or two-part measure, and indicated by the figure 2, thus:

or

When the figures are written like $\frac{2}{2}$ or $\frac{2}{4}$, &c., in the form of a fraction, the upper figure indicates the *kind of measure*, or into how many parts the measure is divided, and the lower figure indicates the kind of note to be used to fill the measure when as many are used as the upper figure suggests. The first part of the measure is accented, and the second part unaccented.

MEASURE AND ACCENT PRACTICALLY ILLUSTRATED.

No. 23.

2d. 1st. 2d. 1st. 2d. 1st. 2d. 1st. 2d. 1st. 2d. 1st. 2d. 1st. 2d. 1st.
Soft. loud. soft. loud. soft. loud. soft. loud. soft. loud. soft. loud. soft. loud. soft. loud.

Oh! let the soul its slum-bers break,—A-rouse its sens-es, and a-wake.

ELEMENTARY INSTRUCTION.

No. 24. What kind of Notes?

Oh! let the soul its slum-bers break,—A - rouse its sens - es, and a - wake.

NOTE 1. After singing Nos. 23 and 24, making the accent well marked, ask the pupils which of the two is better,—more pleasing or satisfactory to the ear.

NOTE 2. It will be observed that the accent of the music must conform to the accent or rhythm of the words.

The parts of the measure may be indicated by counting, or by motions of the hand, called *beating time*. In double measure there are two motions of the hand, or beats (down and up).

No. 25. What kind of measure? What kind of notes?

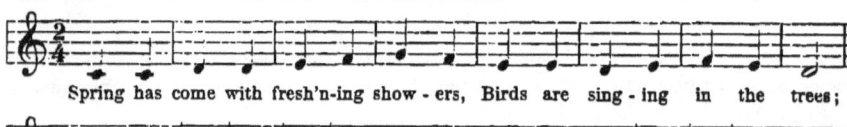

Spring has come with fresh'n-ing show - ers, Birds are sing - ing in the trees;

Hill and val - ley smile with flow - ers, Sweet-est per - fume fills the breeze.

No. 26.

Mu - sic, sweet mu - sic, thy praise we will sing, Plea - sure and hap - pi - ness

SKIP A THIRD.

to us doth bring; Shout, shout a - loud while we make ev' - ry thing Join in the

SKIP A THIRD.   SKIP A FOURTH.

cho - rus, and ech - o voic - es ring. Ring, ring, ring, Ech - o voic - es ring.

No. 27.

We all love one an - oth - er, In our pleas - ant

ELEMENTARY INSTRUCTION.

No. 32.

TRIPLE MEASURE has three parts. The first part is accented.

EXAMPLES.

One, two, three. One, two, three. One, two, three.
Loud, soft, soft. Loud, soft, soft. Loud, soft, soft.
Down, left, up.   Down, left, up.   Down, left, up.

No. 33.

A dot after a note, thus (𝅘𝅥.), or thus (𝅘𝅥.), or thus (𝅘𝅥.), adds one half to the value of the note. If two dots follow the note, thus (𝅗𝅥..), the second dot adds half as much as the first. Dots also have the same effect when placed after a rest.

No. 34. Two parts. **OVER HILL AND VALLEY.**

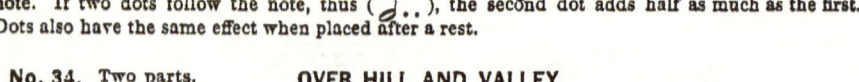

1. O'er hill and val-ley, Riv-er and sea, Now comes the day-king, Rul-ing the day.
2. Wake! wake! ye sleepers, Rise with the sun, Work while the day lasts, Night soon will come.

No. 35. **EVENING.**

Welcome, sweet rest! Day's work is done; Gent-ly and joy-ful-ly Thou dost re-turn.

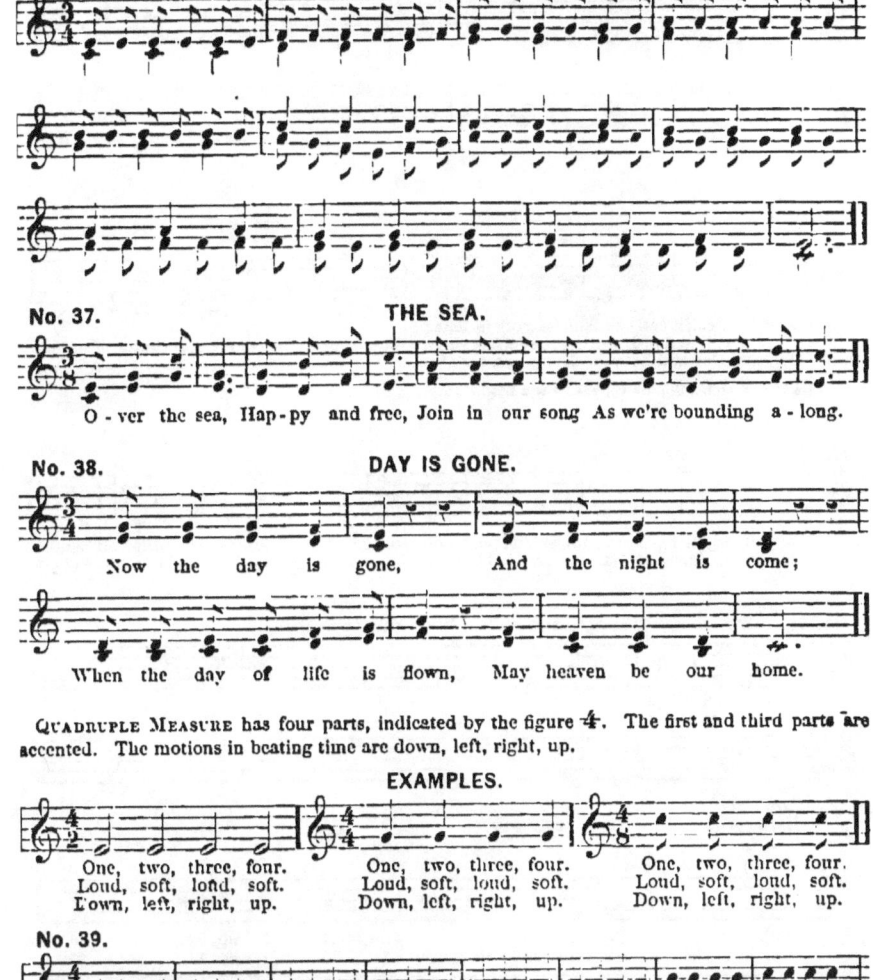

ELEMENTARY INSTRUCTION.

No. 40. Two parts.

No. 41. SATURDAY EVENING.

{ Now the week is end-ed, And its work is done; }
{ All is still and peaceful As the setting sun; } { Earthly joys departing, Leave the tranquil soul,
D. C. Tho'ts of God and heaven, Ev'ry heart control.

DA CAPO, or D. C., means repeat to the beginning.

No. 42.

Do, mi, sol, mi, re, fa, mi, mi, sol, do, si, la, do, sol, re, do, si, la, sol, fa, mi, re, mi, re, do.
la, la, la, la, la, la, la, la, la, la, la, la, la, la, la, la, la, la, la, la, la, la, la, la, la, la.

No. 43. Exercise written upon two staffs. What kind of rests?

ELEMENTARY INSTRUCTION.

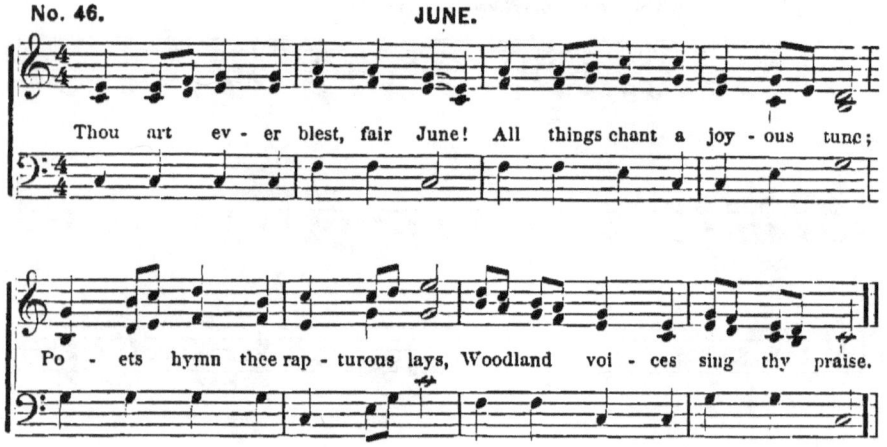

Sometimes three notes are sung in the time of two of the same kind. When this change is made in the value of notes, they are called TRIPLETS, and the figure 3 is usually placed over or under them, thus: ♩♩♩ are equal to ♩♩; ♪♪♪ are equal to ♪♪ &c.

EXERCISE CONTAINING TRIPLETS.

ELEMENTARY INSTRUCTION.   23

CHAPTER VI.

EXPRESSION.

The following words or their abbreviations, and signs, indicate different degrees of force. PIANISSIMO, or *pp*, very soft. PIANO, or *p*, soft. MEZZO PIANO, or *mp*, middling soft. MEZZO, or *m*, medium. MEZZO FORTE, or *mf*, middling loud. FORTE, or *f*, loud. FORTISSIMO, or *ff*, very loud. CRESCENDO, or *cres.*, or <, increase gradually. DIMINUENDO, or *dim.*, or >, decrease gradually. SWELL, < >, increase and diminish. SFORZANDO, or *sfz*,—FORZANDO, or *fz*, or >, or ∧, very strong accent, and suddenly diminish. DOLCE signifies soft and sweet.

TIME is indicated by such words as LENTO (slow); MODERATO (moderate); ALLEGRO (fast), &c.

No. 48.

Dol - ce, soft - ly, sweet - ly sing; Mez - zo, loud - er swell the song; Mezzo For - te,

Loud - er now; Double Forte, ve - ry strong. Still con - tin - ue ve - ry loud, Till by signs it

soft - er grows; Then di - min - ish with great care, Till we reach a soft re - pose.

No. 49. One division of the class may sing the upper notes, and the other the lower, in the following exercise.

ELEMENTARY INSTRUCTION.

SEXTUPLE MEASURE has six parts, indicated by the figure 6⁄ . The different varieties under this head are represented thus:

The accent occurs upon the first and fourth parts of the measure.

No. 50.

No. 51. What kind of measure?

Come, come to the green-wood, Come mer-ri-ly now, Where rip-ple sweet

foun-tains, Where trem-bles the bough; When pass-eth young zeph-yr,

Light dancing a-long, There rus-tles the as-pen, Soft to his sweet song.

No. 52.

No. 53.

1. Far o-ver the east-ern hills of life, A strain floats from the great unknown; It
2. Then soft-ly the ech-oes fold a-way, While words and mu-sic fade again. To

fills the heart with sweet de-light, Which ech-oes back the joy-ful tone.
join the hap-py host a-far, In waves of sound o'er the bound-less plain.

No. 54.   **GOOD MORNING.**

La, la, la, la, la, la, la,   la, la, la, la,   la, la, la, la,
Good morn-ing, good morn-ing, Now hap-py are we;   Night shades have de-

la, la, la, la,   la, la, la, la,   la, la, la, la,   la, la, la, la,
-part-ed; Now joy-ous and free, Join sweet-ly in sing-ing, With voic-es so

la,   la,   la, la, la, la,   la,   la, la, la, la.
clear.   Let   noth-ing dis-cord-ant   Be   practiced while here.

CHAPTER VII.

CHROMATIC SCALE.

Between those tones of the scale which form the interval of a major second, an intermediate tone may be introduced, as between 1 and 2, 5 and 6, &c. Between 3 and 4, or 7 and 8, no tone will occur, as the interval is a minor second.

A Chromatic Interval implies the difference in pitch of two tones represented upon the same degree of the staff, thus:— 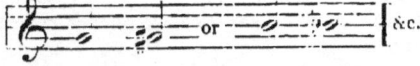 &c.

As there are no more degrees of the staff than have already been used, the intermediate tones must be represented by signs called a SHARP (♯), FLAT (♭), or NATURAL (♮). It will be observed that there are thirteen tones in the chromatic scale, and named ONE, SHARP ONE, TWO, SHARP TWO, &c., thus:—

CHROMATIC SCALE. NAMES AND LETTERS.

ASCENDING.   DESCENDING.

1 ♯1 2 ♯2 3 4 ♯4 5 ♯5 6 ♯6 7 8   8 7 ♭7 6 ♭6 5 ♭5 4 3 ♭3 2 ♭2 1
C C♯ D D♯ E F F♯ G G♯ A A♯ B C   C B B♭ A A♭ G G♭ F E E♭ D D♭ C

The Natural cancels the effect of the sharp or flat, thus:—

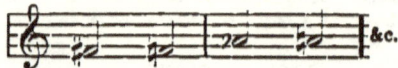

The Double Sharp (𝗑) is used to indicate the next available tone higher than a SINGLE SHARP upon the same degree of the staff; and the Double Flat (♭♭) suggests the next tone lower than a SINGLE FLAT, thus:—

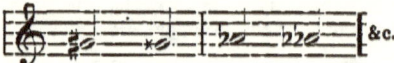

NOTE. In the following exercise the teacher may sing two measures, (excepting at E and F and B and C), and the pupils repeat, making use of the NAMES, LA, and SYLLABLES, at pleasure.

No. 55.

As a rule, the sharp or flat occurring incidentally has no effect out of the measure in which it is found. Its effect may continue through other measures if no note intervenes upon some other degree.

No. 56.

CHAPTER VIII.

THE MINOR SCALE.

Two scales, the major and chromatic, have already been explained. One more remains to be explained, called the MINOR SCALE. This differs from the others in respect to the intervals.

There are two forms, called HARMONIC and MELODIC, as illustrated below. Six (la) of the major is taken for ONE of the minor; it is then called the RELATIVE MINOR (related to).

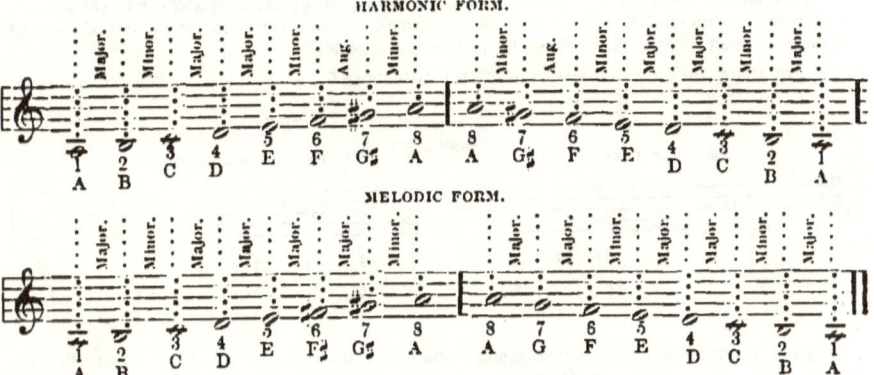

In the harmonic form the minor seconds occur between 2 and 3, 5 and 6, 7 and 8; in the melodic, between 2 and 3, 7 and 8.

No. 57. Key of A minor. **NIGHT WINDS.**

1. The wea-ry night winds are humming low, Their pen-sive me-lo-di-ous strain; They mourn-ful-ly sigh and plain-tive-ly blow, A mi-nor and soft, sad re-frain.

CHAPTER IX.

TRANSPOSITION.

When any other letter than C for the MAJOR and A for the MINOR SCALE is taken for ONE, the Scale is said to be TRANSPOSED. Hence, to transpose the scale is to change its position upon the staff,—place it higher or lower. The scale may be written in any key, or any letter taken for one.

The order of intervals (seconds,) as heretofore learned,—viz: Minor between 3 and 4, and 7 and 8, (Major scale) must, of course, be preserved; and as the Minor seconds occur between the tones (or degrees) E and F, and B and C, it will be found necessary to make use of SHARPS or FLATS to effect this agreement with the letters when the scale is transposed; in other words, make use of some of the intermediate tones which are found in the Chromatic scale.

The first transposition is to take G, (which is a fifth above C,) as One.

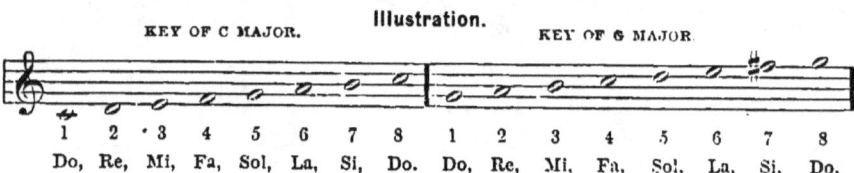

It will be observed that in the above example the tone F sharp is used instead of the tone F. This is because the SECOND from F to G is MAJOR, and to make it MINOR, as from 7 to 8, (as it must always be,) F♯ is substituted.

In each succeeding transposition, by sharps, an additional sharp will be required for 7 of the scale, for the reason above stated.

The number of sharps or flats used are placed at the beginning of a piece of music, immediately after the Clefs, and are called the SIGNATURE, (sign of the key).

ELEMENTARY INSTRUCTION.

No. 58. What key? Why? The signature? Which letter is sharped? Why?

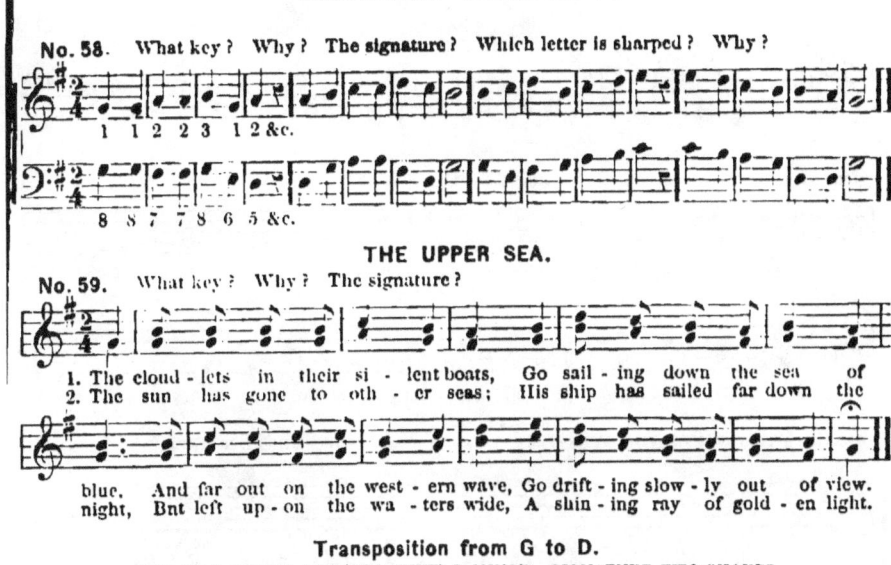

THE UPPER SEA.

No. 59. What key? Why? The signature?

1. The cloud-lets in their si-lent boats, Go sail-ing down the sea of blue. And far out on the west-ern wave, Go drift-ing slow-ly out of view.
2. The sun has gone to oth-er seas; His ship has sailed far down the night, But left up-on the wa-ters wide, A shin-ing ray of gold-en light.

Transposition from G to D.

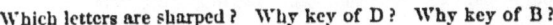

KEY OF D MAJOR AND (RELATIVE) B MINOR. SIGNATURE TWO SHARPS.

Which letters are sharped? Why key of D? Why key of B?

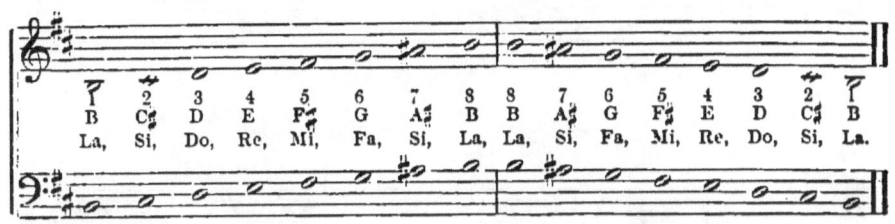

30 ELEMENTARY INSTRUCTION.

No. 60.

No. 61.   **BEAUTIFUL SNOW.**

Beau - ti - ful snow! Beau - ti - ful snow! Fall - ing so light - ly,

Dai - ly and night - ly, Chil - dren de - light in the beau - ti - ful snow.

KEY OF A MAJOR AND (THE RELATIVE) F♯ MINOR. SIGNATURE THREE SHARPS, F♯, C♯ AND G♯.

1	2	3	4	5	6	7	8	8	7	6	5	4	3	2	1
A	B	C♯	D	E	F♯	G♯	A	A	G♯	F♯	E	D	C♯	B	A
Do,	Re,	Mi,	Fa,	Sol,	La,	Si,	Do,	Do,	Si,	La,	Sol,	Fa,	Mi,	Re,	Do.

1	2	3	4	5	6	7	8	8	7	6	5	4	3	2	1
F♯	G♯	A	B	C♯	D	E♯	F♯	F♯	E♯	D	C♯	B	A	G♯	F♯
La,	Si,	Do,	Re,	Mi,	Fa,	Si,	La,	La,	Si,	Fa,	Mi,	Re,	Do,	Si,	La.

No. 62.

ELEMENTARY INSTRUCTION. 31

EXCELSIOR.

No. 63. What kind of measure? Name letters sharped in the signature.

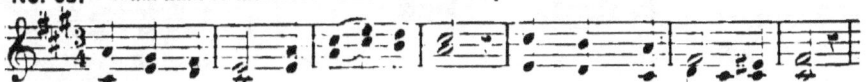

1. Put out thy tal-ents to their use— Lay noth-ing by to rust;
2. So live, in faith and no-ble deed, Till earth re-turns to earth—

Give vul-gar ig - no - rance thy scorn, And in - no - cence thy trust.
So live that men shall mark the time Gave such a mor - tal birth.

KEY OF E MAJOR AND (RELATIVE) C♯ MINOR. SIGNATURE FOUR SHARPS.

What letters are sharped?

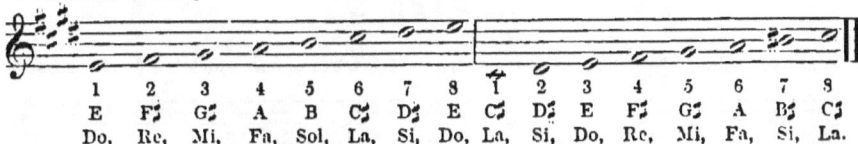

1	2	3	4	5	6	7	8	1	2	3	4	5	6	7	8
E	F♯	G♯	A	B	C♯	D♯	E	C♯	D♯	E	F♯	G♯	A	B♯	C♯
Do,	Re,	Mi,	Fa,	Sol,	La,	Si,	Do,	La,	Si,	Do,	Re,	Mi,	Fa,	Si,	La.

No. 64. What key? Why?

Do, do, re, re, &c.

Do, do, si, si, &c.

No. 65. DA CAPO, or D. C., signifies return to the beginning. FINE signifies the end. DAL SEGNO, or D. S., signifies repeat to the sign (𝄋).

ELEMENTARY INSTRUCTION.

No. 66.   **MANHOOD.**

Rise to thy prop - er place in life, Trample up - on all sin;
But still the gen - tle hand hold out To help the wand'r - er in.

B Major, five sharps (F♯, C♯, G♯, D♯, A♯).   F♯ Major, six sharps (F♯, C♯, G♯, D♯, A♯, E♯).

CHAPTER X.

First transposition of the scale by fourths; that is, F is taken as one, which is a fourth above C.

1   2   3   4   5   6   7   8   1   2   3   4   5   6   7   8

By examining the seconds in the above diagram, taking F as the starting point, or as ONE, it will be readily understood why it is necessary to substitute B♭ for B, viz.: the second between 3 and 4 must be minor, while from A to B is major.

In every succeeding transposition by the use of flats, one additional flat will be required, for the reasons stated above.

KEY OF F MAJOR.

1	2	3	4	5	6	7	8	8	7	6	5	4	3	2	1
F	G	A	B♭	C	D	E	F	F	E	D	C	B♭	A	G	F
Do,	Re,	Mi,	Fa,	Sol,	La,	Si,	Do,	Do,	Si,	La,	Sol,	Fa,	Mi,	Re,	Do.

KEY OF D MINOR.

1	2	3	4	5	6	7	8	8	7	6	5	4	3	2	1
D	E	F	G	A	B♭	C♯	D	D	C♯	B♭	A	G	F	E	D
La,	Si,	Do,	Re,	Mi,	Fa,	Si,	La,	La,	Si,	Fa,	Mi,	Re,	Do,	Si,	La.

34 ELEMENTARY INSTRUCTION.

"SPEAK KINDLY."

No. 70. What key? Signature? Measure? Time?

Moderato.

1. Speak kind-ly to the err-ing one, And strive his heart to win,
   An act of kindness fit-ly done, May tend to draw } from sin:
2. Then let us to the err-ing one With kind-ness speak al-way,
   For-get-ting not that we, likewise, Have faults as well } as they;

Then do not harsh-ly turn a-way, But for the err-ing work and pray.
And ev-er strive, with all our might, To guide them in the path of right.

KEY OF E♭ MAJOR. Signature three flats (B♭, E♭, A♭), and (relative) C MINOR. Which letters are flatted?

MAJOR.   MINOR.

1	2	3	4	5	6	7	8	1	2	3	4	5	6	7	8
Do	Re	Mi	Fa	Sol	La	Si	Do	La	Si	Do	Re	Mi	Fa	Si	La
E♭	F	G	A♭	B♭	C	D	E♭	C	D	E♭	F	G	A♭	B	C

No. 71. The kind of Measure? Time?

Allegro Moderato.

MORNING.

No. 72. The signature? The kind of measure? Time?

Allegro.

1. How bright this glo-rious morn-ing; The storm has passed a-way; The
2. And tune-ful birds are sing-ing The first glad notes of spring; Their
3. Wake thou, and join the cho-rus, Oh, soul with clouds o'er-cast; While

PART II.

EXERCISES, ROUNDS, &c

IN LIGHT TRIPPING MEASURE. (Round in four parts.)

No. 1. (The 2d or 3d part can be omitted.)   P

IMPROVE THE PASSING HOURS.
THREE-PART CHORUS FOR FEMALE VOICES.
WESTROP.

LITTLE FEET, SO WHITE AND FAIR.

SONG & TWO PART CHORUS.

Words by Mrs. M. A. Kidder. Music by Geo. W. Persley.

1. Lit-tle feet so white and fair, Pattering o'er the pavements
2. When the fier-cest winds do blow, When comes down December's

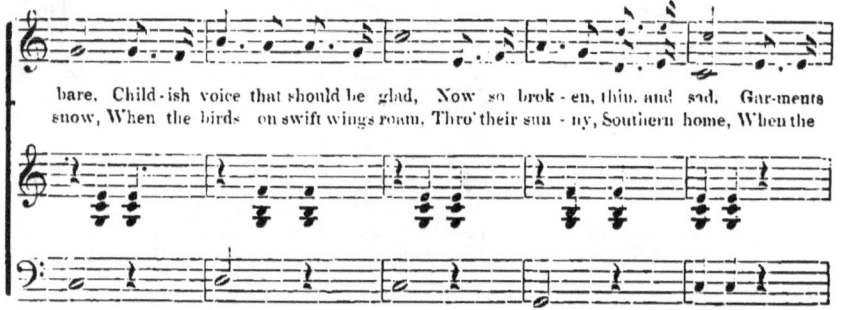

bare, Child-ish voice that should be glad, Now so brok-en, thin, and sad, Gar-ments
snow, When the birds on swift wings roam, Thro' their sun-ny, Southern home, When the

Published in Sheet Music Form. with Lithograph Title page. Price 40 cts.

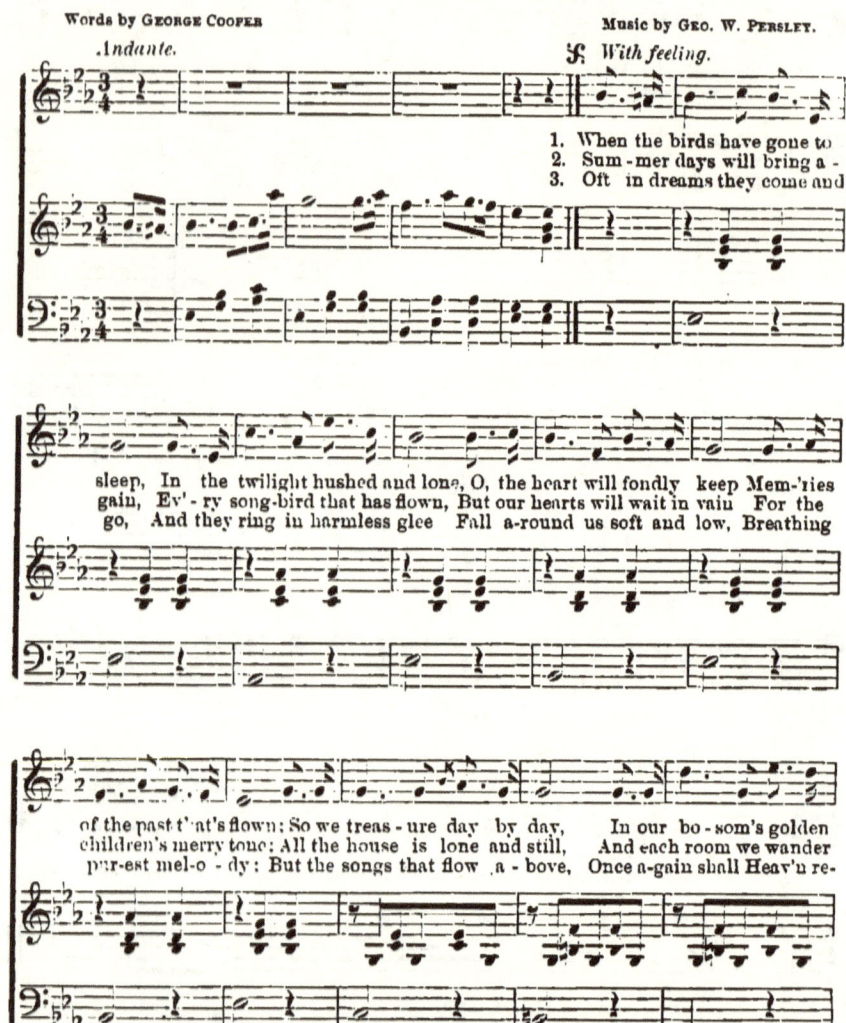

44

No. 22.

LITTLE MAUD.
SONG & CHORUS.

J. P. WEBSTER.

Moderato.

1. Oh yes, she is dain-ty, our dar-ling! The dain-ti-est dar-ling of all; Oh, sweet is her voice on the stair-way, O sweet is her voice in the hall; The pat-ter-ing steps on the en-try. The sil-ver-y laugh in the hall; O here is our dain-ty, our

2. The peach-es are ripe in the gar-den, The a-pri-cots rea-dy to fall; The blue grapes are dripping their hon-ey, In sunshine up-on the white wall: But sweet-er than flow'rs of the sum-mer, Or fruits of the boun-te-ous fall,— Our fai-ry, our beau-ty, our

Published in Sheet Music Form. price 50 cts.

LITTLE MAUD.

BEAUTIFUL FLOWERS FOR MY MOTHER. Concluded.

I AM HAPPY, MOTHER DARLING.

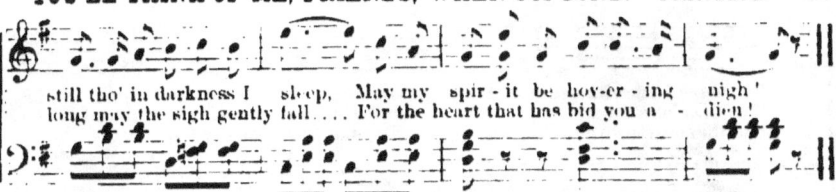

MY SISTER IN HEAVEN.
SONG & TWO-PART CHORUS.

GORHAM.

Moderato.

1. Softly sigh, O light-winged breezes, Floating o'er the per-fumed lea; Breathe a dirge in mourn-ful measure, Sweet as an-gel's min-strel-sy; For a heav'n-loaned star has fad-ed From the house-hold sky it blest,
2. Bright her eyes as cloud-less morning, Ah! how soon to fade in death! Fair her cheeks as Ai-den's ro-ses, Nodding to the mild wind's breath. And her sil-ver laugh-ter ring-ing, Now on earth no more is heard,
3. Yes, we miss thee, earth's lost angel, With thy countless win-some ways— Miss thy pleas-ant smiles and greetings, Heart-gems bright of oth-er days; But we know that ser-aphs bore thee To the ev-er-shin-ing shore,

Published in Sheet Music Form. price 30 cts.

MY SISTER IN HEAVEN. Concluded.

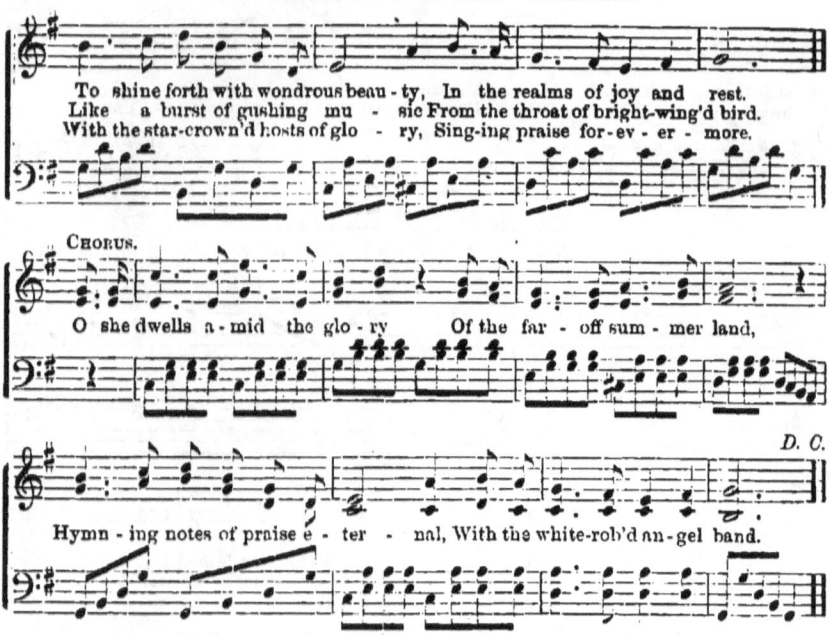

To shine forth with wondrous beau-ty, In the realms of joy and rest.
Like a burst of gushing mu-sic From the throat of bright-wing'd bird.
With the star-crown'd hosts of glo-ry, Sing-ing praise for-ev-er-more.

CHORUS.

O she dwells a-mid the glo-ry Of the far-off sum-mer land,

D. C.

Hymn-ing notes of praise e-ter-nal, With the white-rob'd an-gel band.

PAPA, STAY HOME, I'M MOTHERLESS NOW.

SONG.

WILL. S. HAYS.

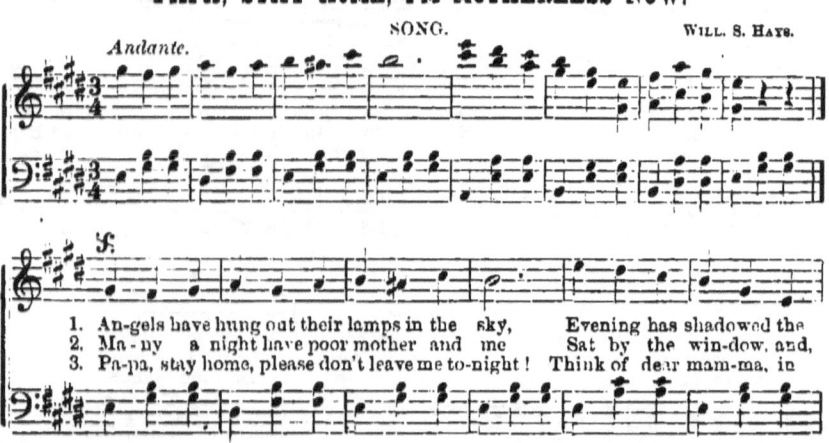

Andante.

1. An-gels have hung out their lamps in the sky, Evening has shadowed the
2. Ma-ny a night have poor mother and me Sat by the win-dow, and,
3. Pa-pa, stay home, please don't leave me to-night! Think of dear mam-ma, in

Published in Sheet Music Form. Price 30 cts.

NOBODY'S DARLING.

SONG.

WILL. S. HAYS.

1. Out in this cold world a-lone,..... Walking a-bout in the street!....
2. No one to kiss me good-night,... No one to put me to bed!......
3. Oft-en at night, when I kneel,... Lifting my sorrow-ful eyes,......

Ask-ing a penny for bread,.... Begging for something to eat,......
Out on the pavement a-lone,..... Weeping for those who are dead,....
Ask-ing my mother to smile,.... Down on her child from the skies,....

Published as a Song & Chorus in Sheet Music Form, with Lithograph Title. Price 40 cts.

OH NO, NOT SAD.

SONG.

T. BRIGHAM BISHOP.

Published in Sheet Music Form, Price 40 cts.

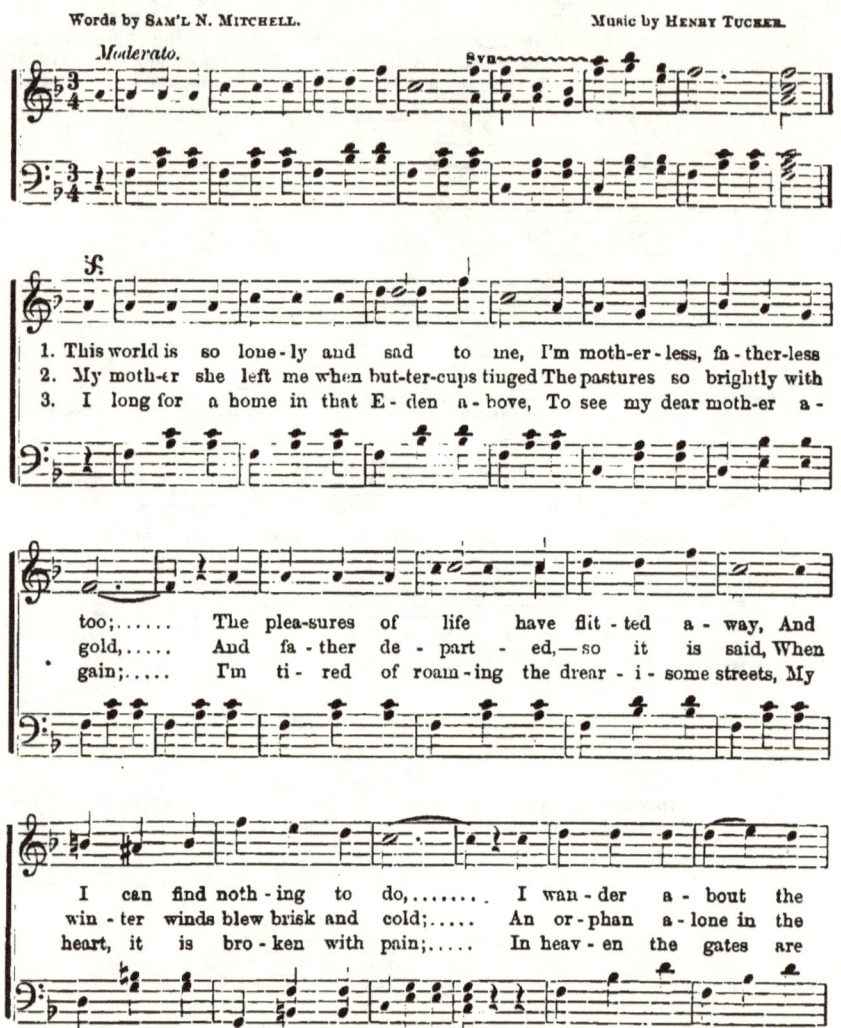

THE LITTLE BROWN CHURCH.
SONG & CHORUS.

WM. S. PITTS.

Published in Sheet Music Form, Price 30 cts.

LET US EVER BE HAPPY. Concluded.

LET US SING MERRILY.

TWO-PART CHORUS.   WESTROP.

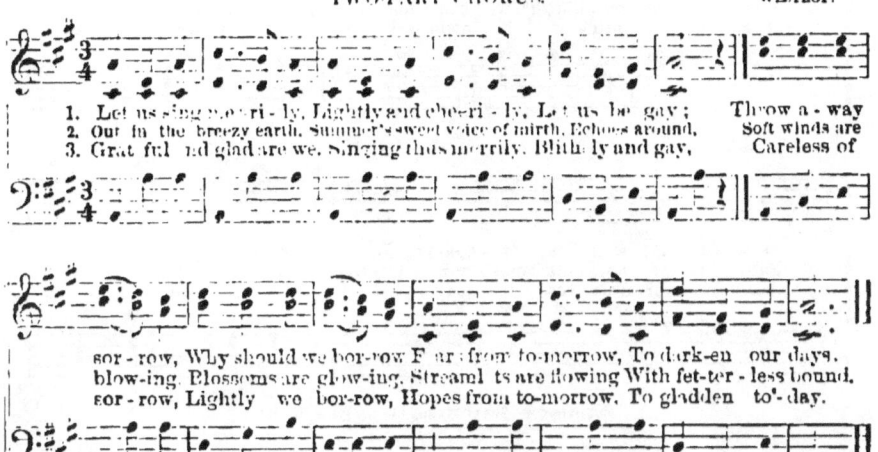

LIST TO THE CONVENT BELLS.

NOTTURNO FOR ONE OR TWO VOICES & CHORUS. (*Tenor & Bass, ad lib.*)

JOHN BLOCKLEY.

LIST TO THE CONVENT BELLS. Concluded.

GOOD NIGHT. Concluded.

THE CORONATION SONG. Concluded.

part - ing hour, Like dew shall gleam on ev' - ry flow'r.
fad - ing flow'r They'll come to glad your ev' - ry hour.
life's dark stream, Like pur - est gems, shall bright - ly gleam.
ra - ven wing, No sha - dow o'er their sun - shine fling.
love you now, Who twined these crowns to grace your brow.

THREE-PART CHORUS.

1ST & 2D SOPRANO.

Re - turn fair girls, to friends and home For love will hail your

ALTO.

Acc.

glad re - turn. *Sym.*

GOOD BYE, TILL I SEE YOU AGAIN. Concluded.

IN THE GRAVE-YARD SOFTLY SLEEPING.

DUET.

Wesley Martin.

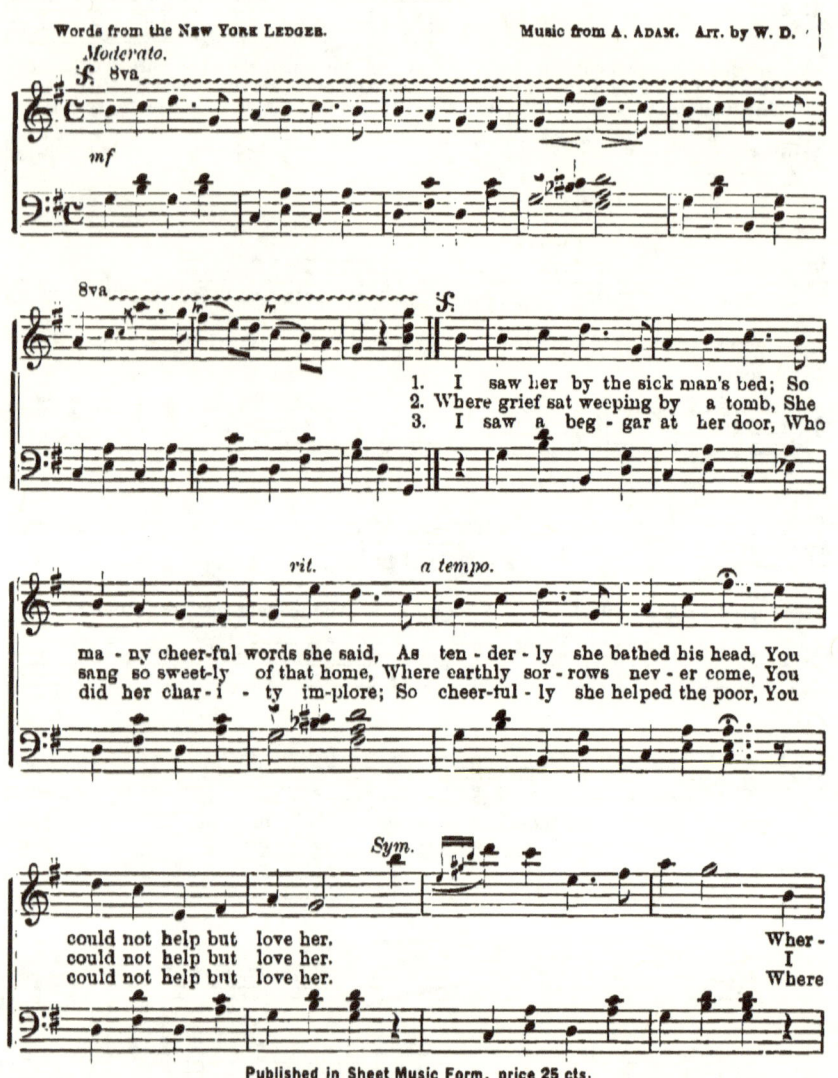

YOU COULD NOT HELP BUT LOVE HER.

JUDGE NOT, THERE'S PARDON FOR US ALL.

SONG.

L. S. Cox.

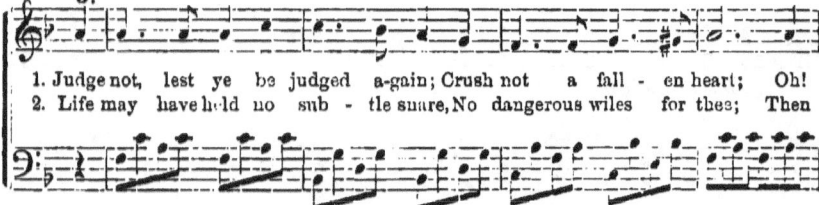

1. Judge not, lest ye be judged a-gain; Crush not a fall-en heart; Oh!
2. Life may have held no sub-tle snare, No dangerous wiles for thee; Then

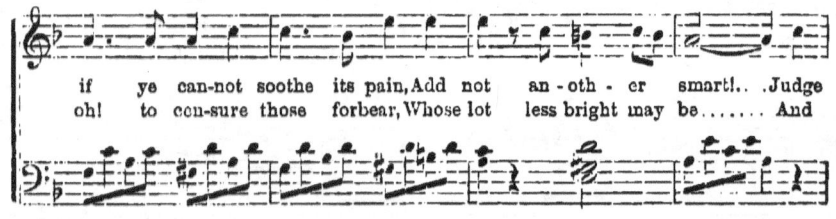

if ye can-not soothe its pain, Add not an-oth-er smart!...Judge
oh! to cen-sure those forbear, Whose lot less bright may be....... And

JUDGE NOT, THERE PARDON FOR US ALL. Concluded.

DO RIGHT AND FEAR NOT. Concluded.

Shadows that surround thee O! soon shall pass a - way.
Life or Death un - fear - ing, Since thou hast done His will.

Chorus.

Do ye right and fear not! In doubt and pain and loss;

Tenor & Bass, ad lib.
Acc.

Onward! thou shalt con-quer, Thou sol-dier of the cross!

O JESUS! WHO FOR LOVE OF ME.
(Verse which may be sung by the children at the Stations of the Cross.)

BEETHOVEN.

Slow and Plaintive.

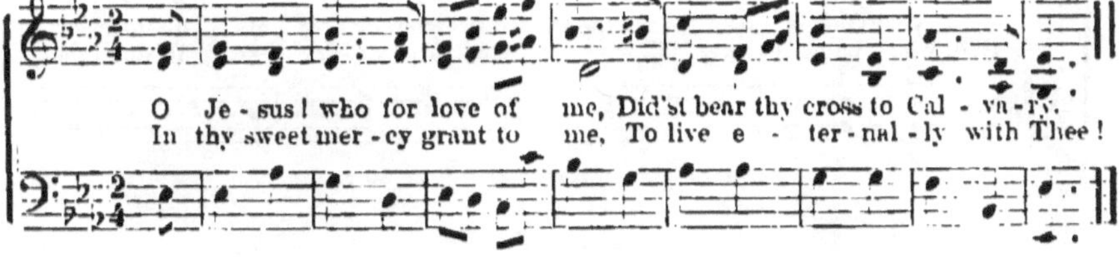

O Je - sus! who for love of me, Did'st bear thy cross to Cal - va - ry.
In thy sweet mer - cy grant to me, To live e - ter - nal - ly with Thee!

HE WIPES THE TEAR FROM EVERY EYE. Concluded.

still your God is near, To wipe the tear from ev - 'ry eye.
God, whose name is love, Will wipe the tear from ev - 'ry eye.

SEEK, AND YE SHALL FIND.

FOR ONE OR TWO VOICES & CHORUS. *Tenor & Bass ad lib.*

Words by GEO. COOPER.   Music by BRIGHAM BISHOP.

Andantino sostenuto.

SOLO OR DUET.

1. Oh! wea - ry souls that on - ward creep, In dark-ness and in pain: O!
2. The bliss ye crave is near at hand, While blindly ye may stray! Thy
3. A land of rest from all thy care; A home of pure de - light! An

hearts that droop with sor - rows deep, In sun-light and in rain: Be -
Sav - iour leads thee to the land, Sweet land of per - fect day! Thy
end of all the grief ye share, O! these are near our sight! Have

Published in Sheet Music Form. Price 30 cts.

FEAR NOT, BUT TRUST IN PROVIDENCE. Concluded.

"Desire of Heaven. Concluded.

THE YOKE OF CHRIST.

TWO or FOUR VOICES.   PLEYEL.

TAKE ME, MY JESUS.
DUET & TWO OR FOUR-PART MIXED CHORUS.

1. Take me, my Jesus, to heaven, To the land of unchange-a-ble love; Let wings to my spir-it be giv-en, To soar to my country a-bove. I'm wea-ry of life, and would fain All its joys and its sorrows now leave; I'd flee from this val-ley of pain, Bliss e-ter-nal from Thee to re-ceive. Then take me, my Je-sus, then take me to heav-en, O

2. How long in this val-ley of tears Shall I lin-ger, an ex-ile from Thee? O, when from the dan-gers and fears That surround, shall my spir-it be free? When death shall release me at last, And my soul shall from earth wing its way, When the dream of this life shall be past, And I'll wake in e-ter-ni-ty's day. Then take, etc.

"Take Me, my Jesus." Concluded.

take me, my Jesus, O take me to heav-en.

PRAY FOR THE DEAD.

QUARTET. W. DRESSLER.

1. Pray for the Dead! at noon and eve.... Lift up to
2. Pray for the Dead! tho' faith-ful they,... Yet while their
3. Pray for the Dead! thy pray'rs, tho' weak,.. May yet be
4. Pray for the Dead in ho-ly fear,... Pray that their

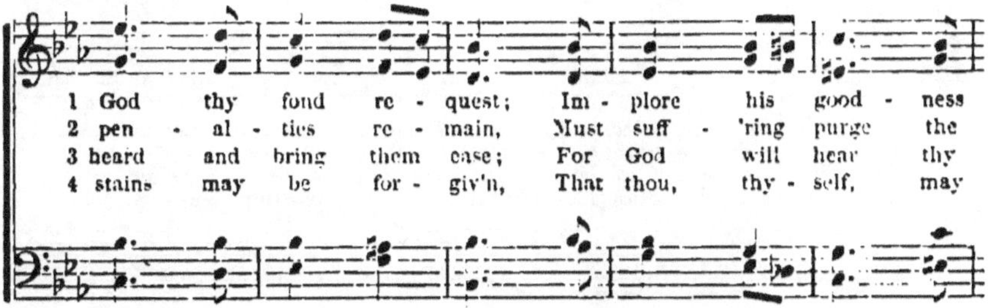

1 God thy fond re-quest; Im-plore his good-ness
2 pen-al-ties re-main, Must suff-'ring purge the
3 heard and bring them ease; For God will hear thy
4 stains may be for-giv'n, That thou, thy-self, may

1 to re-lieve The suff-'ring souls and grant them rest.
2 debt a-way, And pen-ance cleanse the sin-ful stain.
3 sighs, if meek,— Thy tears, if of-fered up for peace.
4 leave the bier, To en-ter pure at once in heav'n.

LORD, TEACH ME HOW TO PRAY.

SONG.

W. V. WALLACE.

1. Lord! teach me how to pray, In - cline my heart to Thee;
2. Oh, frame my lips to speak Words meet for Thee to hear;
3. I would, by day and night, Sweet con-verse hold with Thee;

Grant that I hence-forth may In spir - it more low - ly be.
Long - ing, Thy grace I seek, Oh! drive from my heart all fear.
Guide Thou my tho'ts a - right, That I Thy de - sire may see.

Published in Sheet Music Form. Price 30 cts.

FATHER, EVER KEEP ME NEAR THEE. Concluded. 139

IF YOU LOVE ME, DO MY WILL. Concluded.

THE WILL OF GOD.

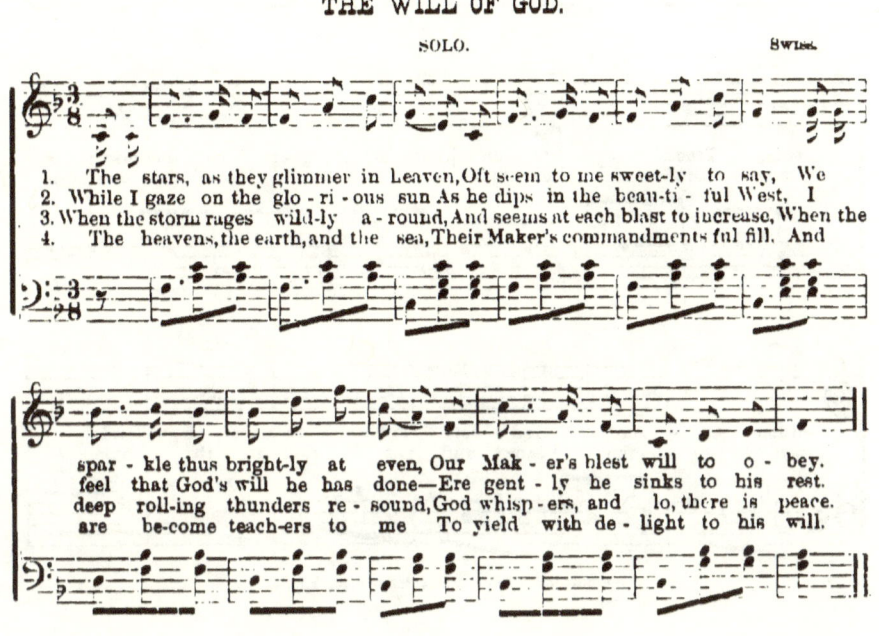

TO THY TEMPLE I REPAIR. Concluded.

GENTLY, LORD, OH! GENTLY LEAD US. Continued.

146 GENTLY, LORD, OH! GENTLY LEAD US. Concluded.

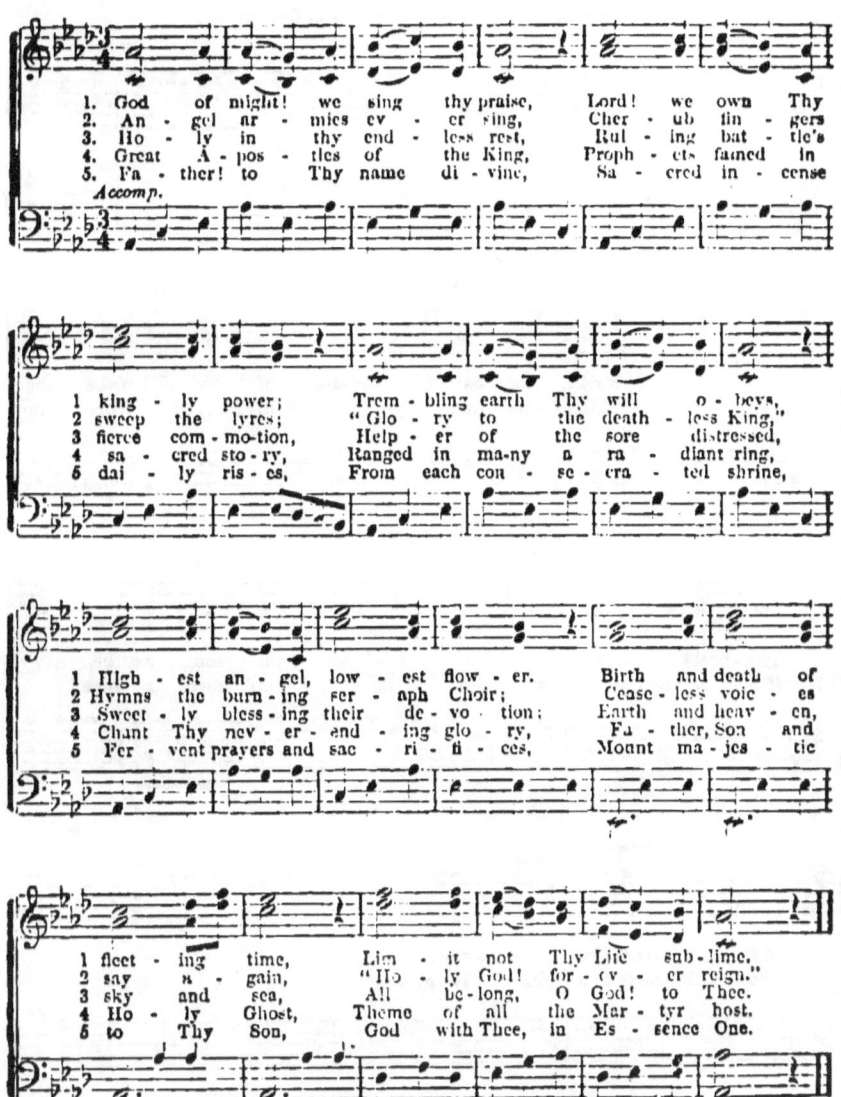

STRIKE THE HARP IN PRAISE OF GOD.

DUET SOLO & CHORUS, *(Tenor & Bass, ad lib.)*

S. NELSON.

1. Strike, the harp in praise of God, Wake the Timbrel's louder mirth, Glorious the song must be, Of the Great Creator's Worth.
2. Honor him ye host of Heav'n! Worship Him ye realms below! Not with outward form alone, But with hearts that purely glow.

Published in Sheet Music Form, Price 30 cts.

STRIKE THE HARP IN PRAISE OF GOD. Concluded.

DUET and TWO-PART CHORUS.

Music by LAMBILLOTTE.

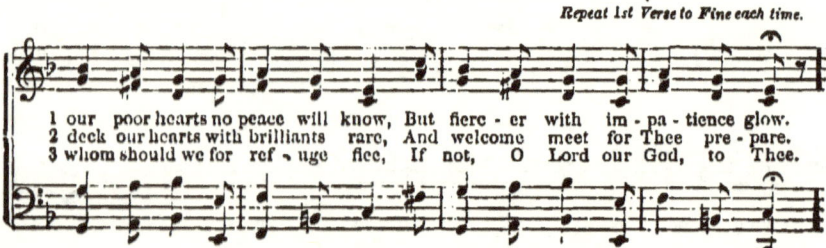

"Hymn for Advent." Concluded.

CHORUS.

Come, O Divine Messiah! Oh, haste, we're weary waiting thee, On earth we nought desire, Save Thee, sweet One in Three.

CREATOR ALME SIDERUM.

Vesper Hymn for the Sundays in Advent.

DUET or TWO-PART CHORUS, or QUARTET — GREGORIAN.

1. Creator alme siderum, Aeterna lux credentium,
2. Qui daemonis ne fraudibus, Periret orbis, impetu,
3. Commune qui mundi nefas Ut expiares, ad crucem,
4. Cujus potestas gloriae, Nomen quum primum sonat;
5. Te deprecamur ultimae, Magnum diei Judicem,
6. Virtus, honor, laus, gloria, Deo Patri cum Filio,

1 Jesu Redemptor omnium, Intende votis supplicum.
2 Amoris actus, languidi, Mundi medela factus es.
3 E Virginis Sacrario, Intacta prodis victima.
4 Et coelites, et infero, Tremente curvantur genu.
5 Armis supernae gratiae, Defende nos ab hostibus.
6 Sancto simul Paraclito, In saeculorum saecula. A-men.

English words may be found in "Peters' Catholic Melodist."

SEE! AMID THE WINTER'S SNOW.

DUET AND 2 OR 4 PART CHORUS. — DOWLAND.

6.
Teach, oh teach us, holy Child,
By Thy face so meek and mild,
Teach us to resemble Thee
In Thy sweet humility! Cho.

7.
Virgin Mother! Mary blest;
By the joys that fill thy breast,
Pray for us, that we may prove
Worthy of the Saviour's love. Cho.

154 ADESTE FIDELES. No. 1. (O Come, all ye Faithful.)

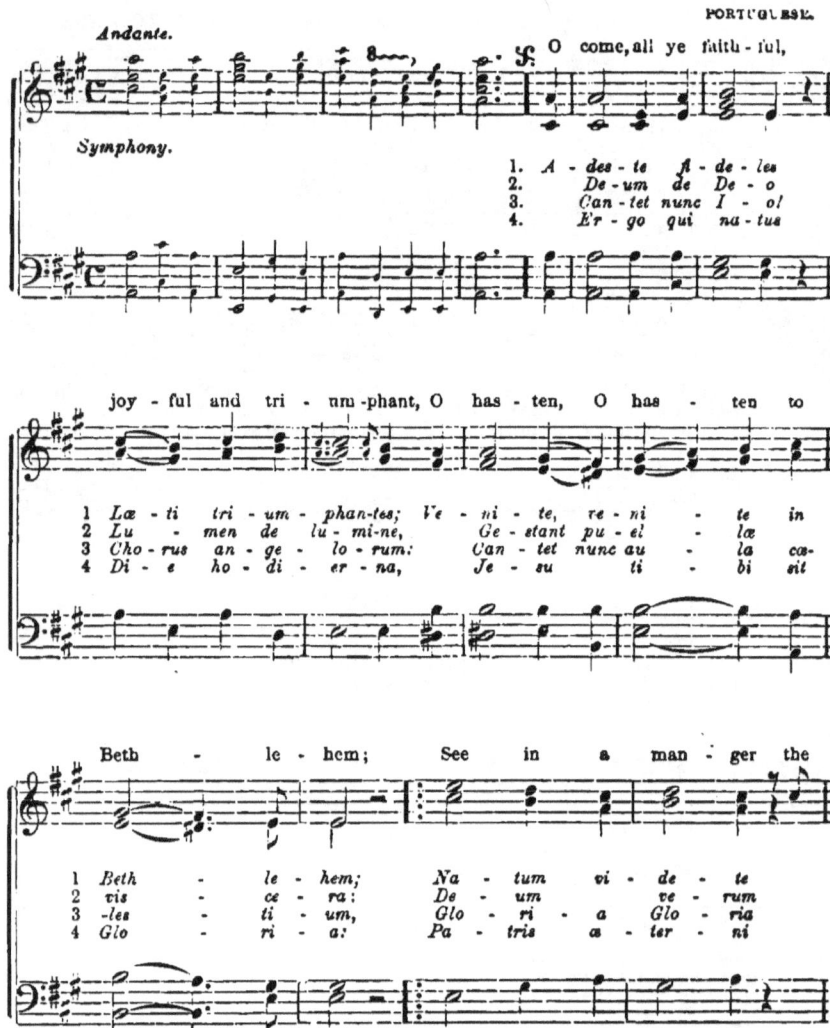

A full and elaborate copy of the universal Hymn is published by J. L. Peters. Price 60 cts.

"Adeste Fideles." No. 1. Concluded.

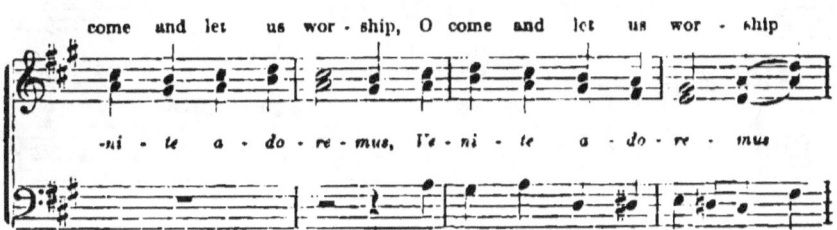

2 God to God equal,
Light of Light eternal,
Lo! he abhors not the Vir-
 [gin's womb.
True God of true God,
Begotten, not created.
 O come, etc.

3 Sing, choirs of angels,
Sing in exultation;
Sing, all ye citizens of Heav-
 [en above.
Glory to God,
Glory in the highest.
 O come, etc.

4 Yea, Lord, we greet thee,
Born this happy morning;
Jesus, to Thee be glory
 [given.
Word of the Father,
Now in flesh appearing.
 O come, etc.

Other Christmas Hymns and Carols are published in a little book entitled "Christmas Chimes." Price 30 cents, or $15 per hundred.

156 COME, ALL YE FAITHFUL. (Adeste Fideles No. 2.)

"Come, all ye Faithful." Concluded.

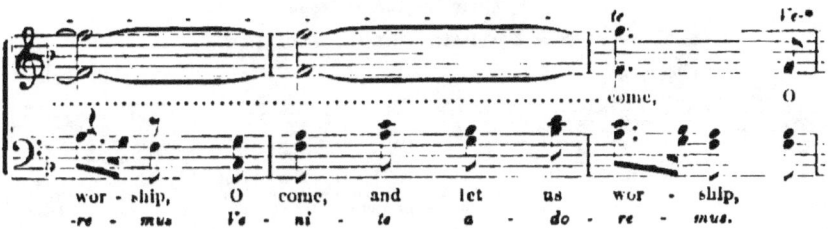

* If sung only by children, or female voices, these *four bars* may be omitted.
The English words may also be sung to the music of Adeste Fideles, No. 1.

    2   3   4

Deum de Deo,   *Cantet nunc Io!*   *Ergo qui natus*
Lumen de Lumine,   *Chorus angelorum:*   *Die hodierna,*
Gestant puellæ viscera;   *Cantet nunc aulá cælestium,*   *Jesu tibi sit gloria,*
  Deum verum,   *Gloria, Gloria*   *Patris æterna*
Genitum non factum: *In excelsis Deo.*   *Verbum caro factum.*
     Venite, etc.   *Venite, etc.*   *Venite, etc.*

"Dear Little One! How Sweet Thou Art." Concluded.

HEART OF THE HOLY CHILD.
DUET OR MIXED QUARTET.

160. JESUS, THE ONLY THOUGHT OF THEE.
SOLO & THREE-PART CHORUS.

Andante espress.

1. Je - sus, the on - ly thought of Thee With sweet - ness fills my breast; But sweet - er far it is to see, And on Thy beau - ty feast; But sweet - er far it is to see, And on Thy beau - ty feast.

2. No sound, no har - mo - ny so gay, Can art of mu - sic frame; No thoughts can reach, no words can say The sweets of Thy blest name; No tho'ts can reach, no words can say The sweets of Thy blest name.

3. No art, nor el - o - quence of man Can tell the joys of love: On - ly the saints can un - der - stand What they in Je - sus love: On - ly the saints can un - der - stand What they in Je - sus prove.

4. Be Thou the ob - ject of our joy, Who our re - ward will be; Be it our glo - ry, our employ, For - ev - er to praise Thee; Be it our glo - ry, our employ, For - ev - er to praise Thee.

JESUS MY GOD, MY ALL. 163

DUET, OR MIXED QUARTET.   Dressler.

1. O Jesus, Jesus! dearest Lord! Forgive me if I say, For
2. O wonderful! that Thou shouldst let So vile a heart as mine, Love
3. For Thou to me art all in all, My honor and my wealth, My

1 very love Thy sacred name A thousand times a day. I
2 Thee with such a love as this, And make so free with Thine. The
3 heart's desire, my body's strength, My soul's eternal health. Burn,

1 love Thee so, I know not how My transports to control; Thy
2 craft of this wide world of ours Poor wisdom seems to me; Oh,
3 burn, Oh love, within my heart, Burn fiercely night and day, Till

1 love is like a burning fire, Within my very soul.
2 dearest Jesus, I have grown Childish with love of Thee.
3 all the dross of earthly love Is burned and burned away.

JESUS AND THE CHILDREN. Concluded.

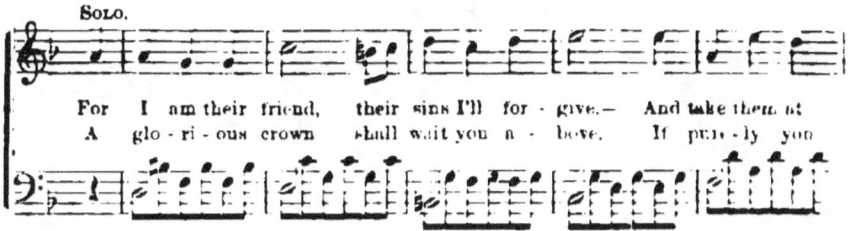

For I am their friend, their sins I'll for-give.— And take them at
A glo-ri-ous crown shall wait you a-bove. If purely you

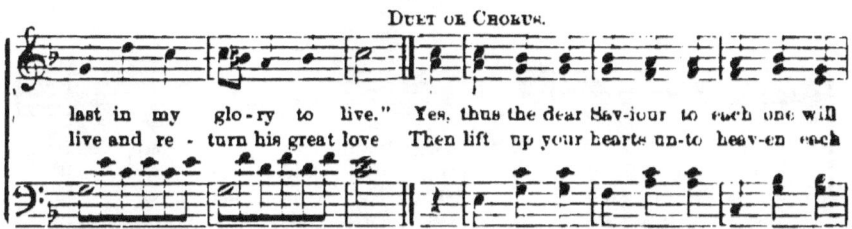

last in my glo-ry to live." Yes, thus the dear Sav-iour to each one will
live and re-turn his great love Then lift up your hearts un-to heav-en each

say, If but from your hearts for a blessing you pray, He'll make your hearts
day, For now and for ev-er the Sav-iour doth say: "Oh, suf-fer the

clean, and he'll teach you His love, And give you a place in His kingdom a-bove.
children to come un-to me. For the kingdom of Heav-en of children shall be."

LOVE OF JESUS.

DUET OR TWO-PART CHORUS.

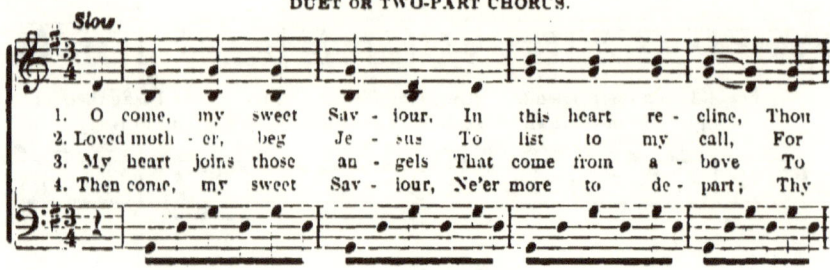

1. O come, my sweet Saviour, In this heart recline, Thou
2. Loved mother, beg Jesus To list to my call, For
3. My heart joins those angels That come from above To
4. Then come, my sweet Saviour, Ne'er more to depart; Thy

1 knowest, my Jesus, 'Twill ever be thine.
2 He is my Saviour, My God, and my all.
3 sing 'round this altar Hosannas of love.
4 home is my bosom, Thy altar my heart.

CHORUS.
O God of love, my soul's sweet delight, Keep

ever thy child From sin's dreary night.

JESUS CRUCIFIED.   169

DUET or MIXED QUARTET.

THE GLORIOUS MYSTERIES. (Easter.)

TWO-PART CHORUS. (with Tenor & Bass ad lib.)

MENDELSSOHN.

1. By the first bright Eas-ter day, When the stone was roll'd a-way; By the glo-ry round Thee shed, At Thy ris-ing from the dead.
2. By Thy part-ing blessing giv'n, As thou did'st as-cend to heav'n; By the cloud of liv-ing light, That re-ceived Thee out of sight.
3. By that rush-ing sound of might, Coming down from heaven's height, By the clo-ven tongue of fire, Ho-ly Ghost our hearts in-spire. } King of
4. See the Vir-gin Moth-er rise, An-gels bear her to the skies, Mount a- loft im-pe-rial queen, Plead on high the cause of men.
5. Ma-ry reigns up-on the throne, Pre-or-dained for her a-lone; Saints and an-gels round her sing, Moth-er of our God and King.

glo-ry hear our cry, Make us soon Thy joys to see, Where en-thron'd in ma-jes-ty, Count-less an-gels sing to Thee. A-men.

172 OUR FATHER. Chant.
GREGORIAN.

1. Our Father, who art in Heaven, Hallowed be Thy name, Thy Kingdom come, Thy will be done on earth as it is in Heaven.
2. Give us this day our daily bread, and forgive us our trespasses as we forgive them that trespass against us.
3. And lead us not into temp-ta - tion, but deliver us from e - vil. A - men.

HAIL MARY. Chant.
GREGORIAN.

1. Hail Mary full of grace, The Lord is with thee.
2. Blessed art thou amongst wo - men, And blessed is the fruit of thy womb, Je - sus
3. Holy Mary Mother of God, Pray for us sinners now, and at the hour of our death. A - men.

ACT OF CONTRITION. Chant.
W. D.

1. O God of Mercy pity us, With weep - ing hearts we cry,
2. My God, because Thou art so good, With sor - row I de - plore

Do Thou then kindly pardon us, And hear Thy children's sigh.
How I offended Thee by sin, I will of - fend no more.

HOLY CHURCH, THOU ART OUR MOTHER. 173

FOR 2 OR 4 VOICES. CROWN OF JESUS.

1. Ho-ly Church, thou art our mother, Nurtur'd in thy bo-som we
Will o-bey thee, for no oth-er Hath e-ter-nal life save thee.
Thou art one, and thou art ho-ly, Spread thro' ev'ry age and clime,
Gov-ern'd by One Shepherd sole-ly, Thou canst brave the force of time.

2. Ho-ly Mother, thou dost feed us With life giv-ing food di-vine,
Thy good pas-tors gently lead us; Ah, what hap-pi-ness is mine.
In thy fold no harm can reach us, Safe beneath thy watchful care;
Gracious Lord, bless those who teach us, Hear thy faithful children's prayer.

174. VENI CREATOR SPIRITUS.

DUET or QUARTET.
Sung before the Sermon.

1. Ve - ni Cre - a - tor Spi - ri - tus! Men - tes tu - o - rum vi - si - ta;
2. Qui di - ce - ris Pa - ra - cli - tus! Al - tis - si - mi do - num De - i;
3. Tu sep - ti - for - mis mu - ne - re! Digi - tus Pa - ter - næ dex - te - ræ;
4. De - o Pa - tri sit Glo - ri - a! Et Fi - li - o qui a mor - tu - is;

1 Im - ple su - per - na gra - ti - a: Quæ tu cre - as - ti pec - to - ra.
2 Fons vi - vus ig - nus cha - ri - tas, Et spi - ri - ta - lis unc - ti - o.
3 Tu ri - te promissum Pa - tris; Ser - mo - ne di - tans gut - tu - ra.
4 Sur - rex - it ac Pa - ra - cli - to; In sæ - cu - lo - rum sæ - cu - la.

COME, O CREATOR, SPIRIT BLEST. (Veni Creator, No. 2.)

1. Come, O Cre - a - tor, Spir - it blest! And in our souls take up thy rest;
2. Great Pa - ra - clete! to Thee we cry; O high - est gift of God most high!
3. Thou in Thy sev'n-fold gifts art known; The fin - ger of God's hand we own;
4. All glo - ry while the a - ges run Be to the Fa - ther and the Son!

1 Come, with Thy grace and heavenly aid, To fill the hearts which Thou hast made.
2 O fount of life! O fire of love! And sweet A - noint - ing from a - bove.
3 The promise of the Fa - ther Thou! Who dost the tongue with power en - dow.
4 Who rose from death; the same to Thee, O Ho - ly Ghost, e - ter - nal - ly.

Either of the tunes may be sung to Latin or English words.

A RULE OF LIFE. Concluded.

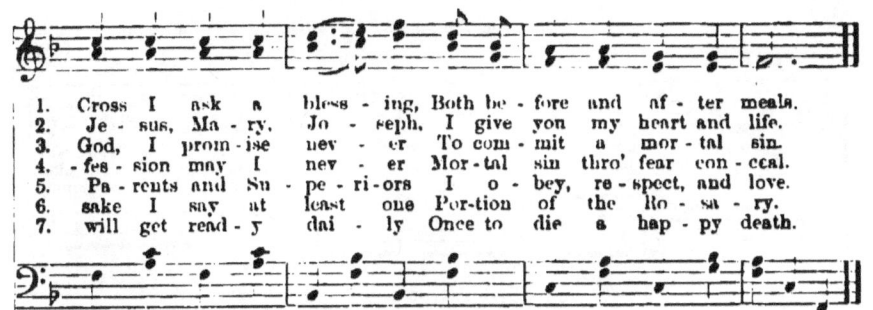

1. Cross I ask a bless - ing, Both be - fore and af - ter meals.
2. Je - sus, Ma - ry, Jo - seph, I give you my heart and life.
3. God, I prom - ise nev - er To com - mit a mor - tal sin.
4. - fes - sion may I nev - er Mor - tal sin thro' fear con - ceal.
5. Pa - rents and Su - pe - ri - ors I o - bey, re - spect, and love.
6. sake I say at least one Por - tion of the Ro - sa - ry.
7. will get read - y dai - ly Once to die a hap - py death.

HAIL! SWEET TEMPERANCE.
DUET OR MIXED QUARTET.
Moderato. HEMY.

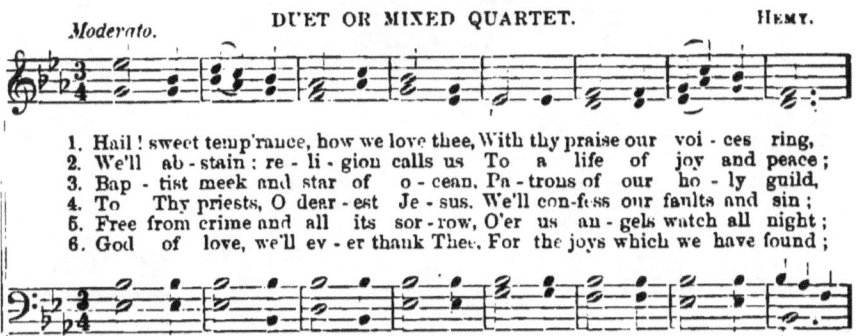

1. Hail! sweet temp'rance, how we love thee, With thy praise our voi - ces ring,
2. We'll ab - stain: re - li - gion calls us To a life of joy and peace;
3. Bap - tist meek and star of o - cean, Pa - trons of our ho - ly guild,
4. To Thy priests, O dear - est Je - sus, We'll con - fess our faults and sin;
5. Free from crime and all its sor - row, O'er us an - gels watch all night;
6. God of love, we'll ev - er thank Thee, For the joys which we have found;

1. And of joys to those who pledge thee Round God's al - tar we will sing.
2. Now no more false friends shall tempt us, Now, O God, our sin shall cease.
3. Hear our pledge, help our de - vo - tion, On our aid our hopes we build.
4. At com - mun - ion Thou wilt bless us, Thus e - ter - nal joys we'll win.
5. Ho - ly Mass comes with each morrow, Bring-ing bless - ings to our sight.
6. Bless Thy guild, we hum - bly ask Thee, Till with peace all hearts a - bound.

EVE OF COMMUNION.

DUET and TWO-PART CHORUS.   LAMBILLOTTE.

1. To-mor-row morn, O joy all words trans-cend-ing, Our God will come in eu-cha-ris-tic guise, Our hearts with His in sweet com-mun-ion blend-ing, Will raptured taste the bliss of Par-a-dise.
2. Now fad-ing fast day's bril-liant rays de-clin-ing, Tell that the morn, the day of love is near, That soon the Sun of jus-tice brightly shin-ing, In mer-cy veiled will to our souls ap-pear.
3. An-oth-er morn will come, too sa-cred seem-ing, When we may say fare-well to mor-tal strife; Haste, haste, that dawn, now in the fu-ture gleaming, The morn that leads us to e-ter-nal life.

CHORUS.

Oh Moth-er loved, our cold hearts pre-pare, Thy Je-sus seeks to make His dwell-ing there; With vir-tues bright thy children's hearts a-dorn, For in their

"Eve of Communion." Concluded.

depths He'll rest to-morrow morn, For in their depths He'll rest to-morrow morn.

(a.) **IN THIS SACRAMENT, SWEET JESUS.**
(b.) **COME, SWEET JESUS.**

CHORUS for TWO or FOUR VOICES. — MOZART.

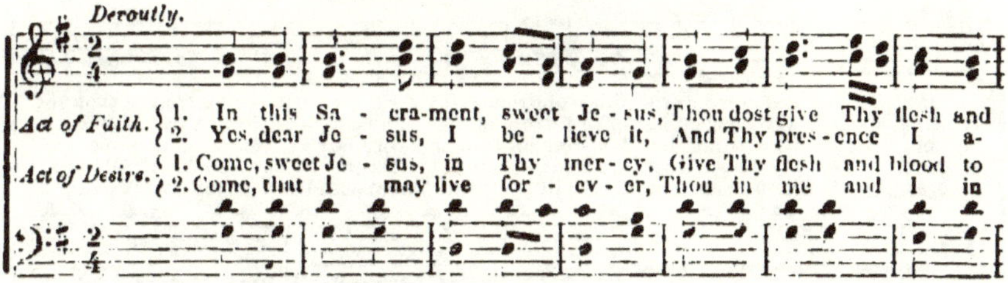

Devoutly.

Act of Faith.
1. In this Sa - cra - ment, sweet Je - sus, Thou dost give Thy flesh and
2. Yes, dear Je - sus, I be - lieve it, And Thy pres - ence I a-

Act of Desire.
1. Come, sweet Je - sus, in Thy mer - cy, Give Thy flesh and blood to
2. Come, that I may live for - ev - er, Thou in me and I in

a.
1 blood, With Thy soul and God - head al - so, As our own most pre-cious food.
2 -dore, And with all my heart I love Thee, May I love Thee more and more.

b.
1 me; Come to me, O dear - est Je - sus, Come, my soul's true life to be.
2 Thee; Liv - ing thus I shall not per - ish, But shall live e - ter - nal - ly.

ACT OF SPIRITUAL COMMUNION. (Chant.)

GREGORIAN.

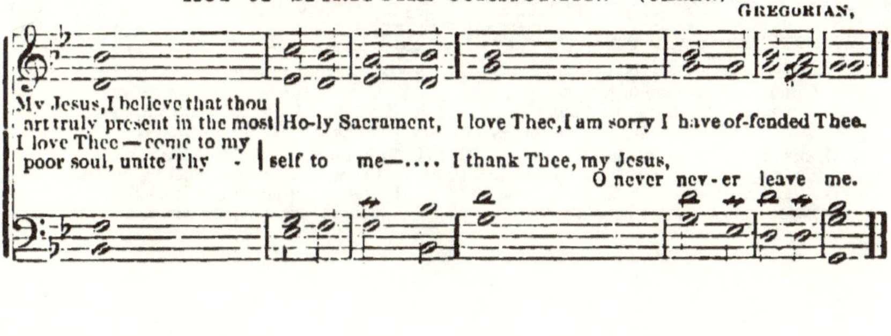

My Jesus, I believe that thou art truly present in the most | Ho-ly Sacrament, I love Thee, I am sorry I have of-fended Thee.
I love Thee — come to my poor soul, unite Thy - | self to me—.... I thank Thee, my Jesus,
O never nev-er leave me.

BLESSED SACRAMENT.

SOLO and TWO-PART CHORUS.

Words by Father Faber.

6 Ye angels, lend your heav'nly tongues;
　Come, and with me in praises join;
　Come, and unite in thankful songs,
　　Your sweet, immortal voice to mine.

7 O, that I had your burning hearts,
　To love my God, my spouse most dear!
　O, that He would, with flaming darts,
　　Raise in my heart a heav'nly fire!

8 Dear Jesus! now my heart is Thine;
　O, may it from Thee never fly!
　Hold it with chains of love divine,
　　Make it be Thine eternally.

9 Vain objects! that seduced my soul,
　I now despise your fleeting charms;
　In vain temptation's billows roll,
　　I lie secure in Jesus' arms.

HOLY COMMUNION.

DUET or TWO-PART CHORUS.

5 Lover of souls! that fondly guardest
The heart from earth's affection free,
And with the bliss of heaven rewardest
The heart that beats ‖: alone for thee : ‖
O, never let another dwell,
Within this breast thou lovest so well.
Sweet, &c.

6 O, bread of Angels! Food of love!
That fill'st the heart with sweetest bliss,
Thou art the rarest boon above,
And what has earth ‖: compared to this: ‖
O, without thee the soul is dead,
Thou art its Life, Celestial Bread.
Sweet, &c.

HYMN FOR CONFIRMATION.
TWO-PART CHORUS. — CZERNY.

1. My God, accept my heart this day, And make it always Thine, That
   I from Thee no more can stray, No more from Thee decline.
2. Before the Cross of Him who died, Behold, I prostrate fall; Let
   ev'ry sin be crucified—Let Christ be all in all.
3. Anoint me with Thy heav'nly grace, Adopt me for Thine own, That
   I may see Thy glorious face, And worship at Thy throne.
4. May the dear blood once shed for me, My blest atonement prove,—That
   I from first to last may be The purchase of Thy love.
5. Let ev'ry thought, and work, and word, To Thee be ever given,—Then
   life shall be Thy service, Lord, And death the gate of heaven.

PRAISE THE LORD. *(Laudate Dominum.)*
CHANT TO BE SUNG AFTER THE BENEDICTION.

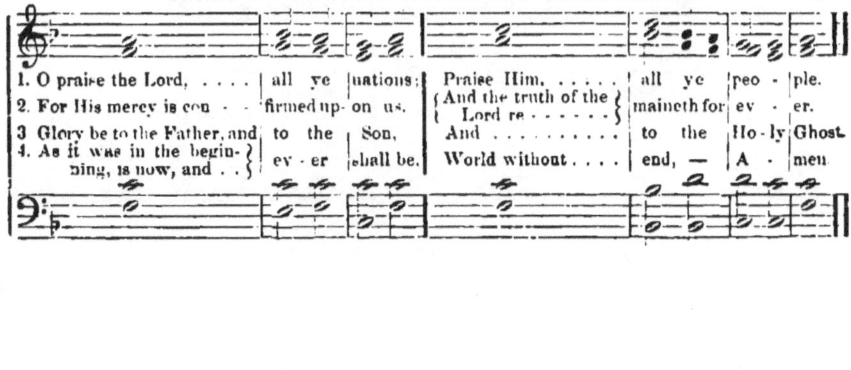

1. O praise the Lord, ... all ye nations; Praise Him, ... all ye people.
2. For His mercy is confirmed upon us. And the truth of the Lord re..... maineth for ever.
3. Glory be to the Father, and to the Son, And .... to the Holy Ghost.
4. As it was in the beginning, is now, and ever shall be, World without .... end,— A men

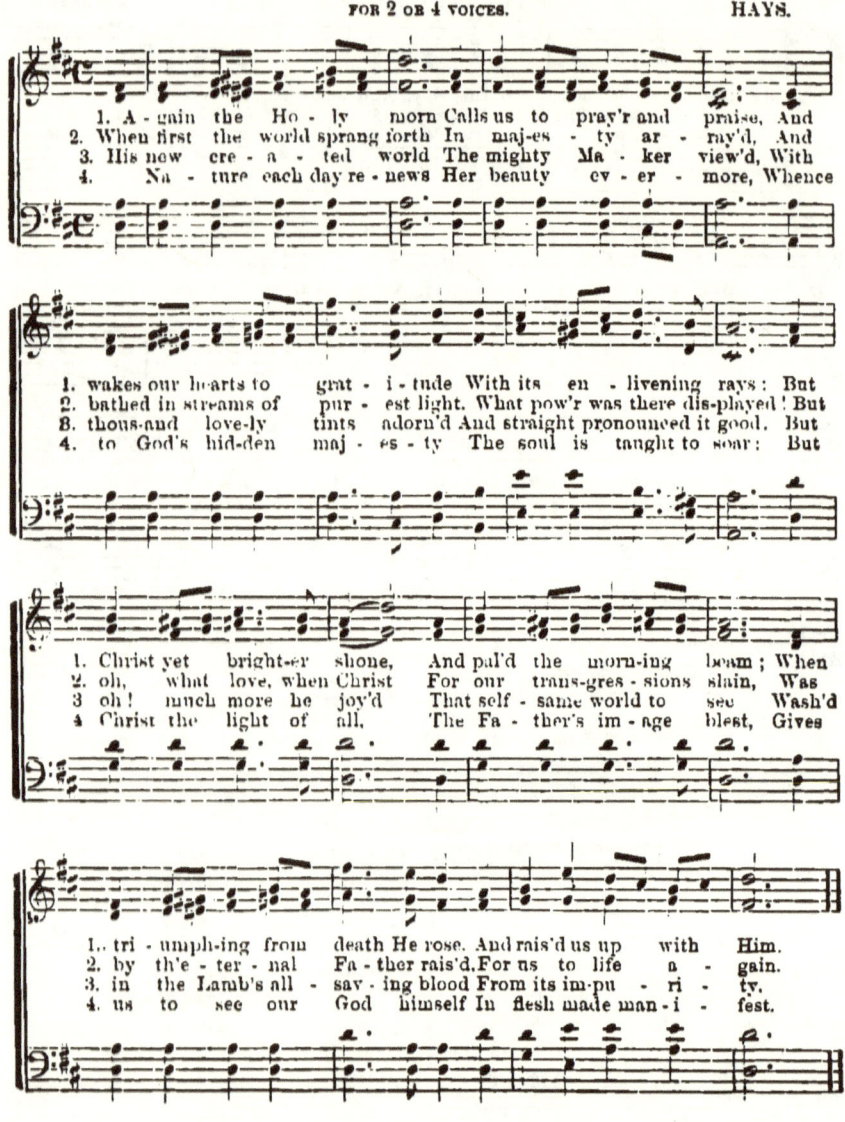

FADING STILL FADING.

(EVENING HYMN.)

SOLO, DUET & THREE-PART CHORUS.

WIEGENTHAL.

FADING STILL FADING. Concluded.

EVENING SONG TO THE VIRGIN.

DUET.

MRS. HEMANS & SISTER.

1. A - ve sanc - tis - si - ma, We lift our souls to Thee;
   O - ra pro no - bis, Thou bright star of the sea.
2. A - ve pu - ris - si - ma, List to thy chil-dren's prayer;
   Au - di Ma - ri - a, And take us to thy care.

EVENING SONG TO THE VIRGIN. Concluded.

EVENING CLOSES. Concluded.

GENTLE STAR OF OCEAN. (Ave Maris Stella.)

DUET or TWO-PART CHORUS.

A - ve Ma - ris Stel - la, De - i Ma - ter al - ma, Atque

1. Gen - tle Star of O - cean, Por - tal of the sky, Ever
2. Oh! by Ga - bri - el's A - ve, Ut - ter'd long a - go, Eva's
3. Break the cap - tive's fet - ters; Light on blind - ness pour; All our
4. Show thy - self a Moth - er; Of - fer Him our sighs, Who for
5. Vir - gin of all Vir - gins! to thy care us take; Gentlest
6. Still as on we jour - ney, Help us in our choice; Till with

sem - per Vir - go, Fe - lix cœ - li por - ta. CHORUS.

1 Vir - gin Mother, Of the Lord most high.
2 name re - versing, 'Stablish peace be - low.
3 ills ex - pelling, Ev - 'ry bliss im - plore.
4 us In - carnate, Did not thee despise.
5 of the gentle! Chaste and gentle us make.
6 Thee and Jesus, Ev - er we re - joice.

E - vi - va Ma - ri - a! Ma -

-ri - a, E - vi - va E - vi - va Ma - ri - a! E chi la cre - o.

THE ANNUNCIATION.

SOLO & DUET or TWO-PART CHORUS.

Words by A. PROCTER. Music by S. N. D.

LITANY OF THE B. V. M. Concluded.

WESLEY.

Chris - te e - lei - son. Chris - te e - lei - son

Chris - te audi - nos, Chris - te ex - audi - nos.
Fili Redemptor mundi De - us, Mise - re - re no - bis.
Sancta Trinitas u-nus De - us, Mise - re - re no - bis.

Sanc-ta Vir - go vir - gi - num, O - ra pro no - bis.

Ma - ter pu - ris - si - ma, O - ra pro no - bis.
Mater in - te - me - ra - ta, O - ra pro no - bis.
Ma - ter cre - a - to - ris, O - ra pro no - bis.
Vir - go ven - e - ran - da, O - ra pro no - bis.
Vir - go cle - mens, O - ra pro no - bis.
Se - des sa - pi - en - ti - ae, O - ra pro no - bis.
Vas hon - o - ra - bi - le, O - ra pro no - bis.
Tur - ris Da - vi - di - ca, O - ra pro no - bis.
Foe - de - ris ar - ca, O - ra pro no - bis.
Sa - lus in - fir - mo - rum, O - ra pro no - bis.
Auxili-um Christian - o - rum, O - ra pro no - bis.
Regi - na pro - phe - ta - rum, O - ra pro no - bis.
Regi - na Con - fes - so - rum, O - ra pro no - bis.
Regina sancto - rum om - ni - um, O - ra pro no - bis.

Regina Sacratissimi Ro - sa - rii, O - ra pro no - bis.

3 Agnus Dei qui tollis peccata mun - di, * Mi - se - re - re no - bis.

R. Ut digni efficiamur promissionibus Christi.

MATER ADMIRABILIS.

(TWO PART SOLO AND CHORUS.)

Music arranged from CONCONE.

MOTHER LOVED.
DUET or TWO-PART CHORUS & SOLO.

Words by S. N. D.
Music by L. LAMBILLOTTE.

"Mother Loved." Concluded.

"Maiden Mother." Concluded.

dy ing words shall be, "Vir - gin Moth - er, pray for me!" Oh

pray for me! Oh pray for me............

O MARY BLEST.

HEMY. "Crown of Jesus."

1. O Ma - ry blest, A moth - er be to me; For who in heav'n or earth can find A
2. Think, Moth-er blest, That thine own Son divine, When nail'd up - on His cross on high For
3. O thou who art In heav'n at His right hand, Obtain that I a-gain may see My

1 mother half so good and kind, So fair, so sweet as thee? So fair, so sweet as thee?
2 me He was a-bout to die, Made thee, His mother, mine, Made thee, His mother, mine.
3 pa-rents dear with Him and thee, In that bright, hap - py land, In that bright, happy land.

MARY QUEEN OF MY SOUL.

Words by Mrs. MONROE.   Solo and 2 part chorus.   Music by WOLLASTON.

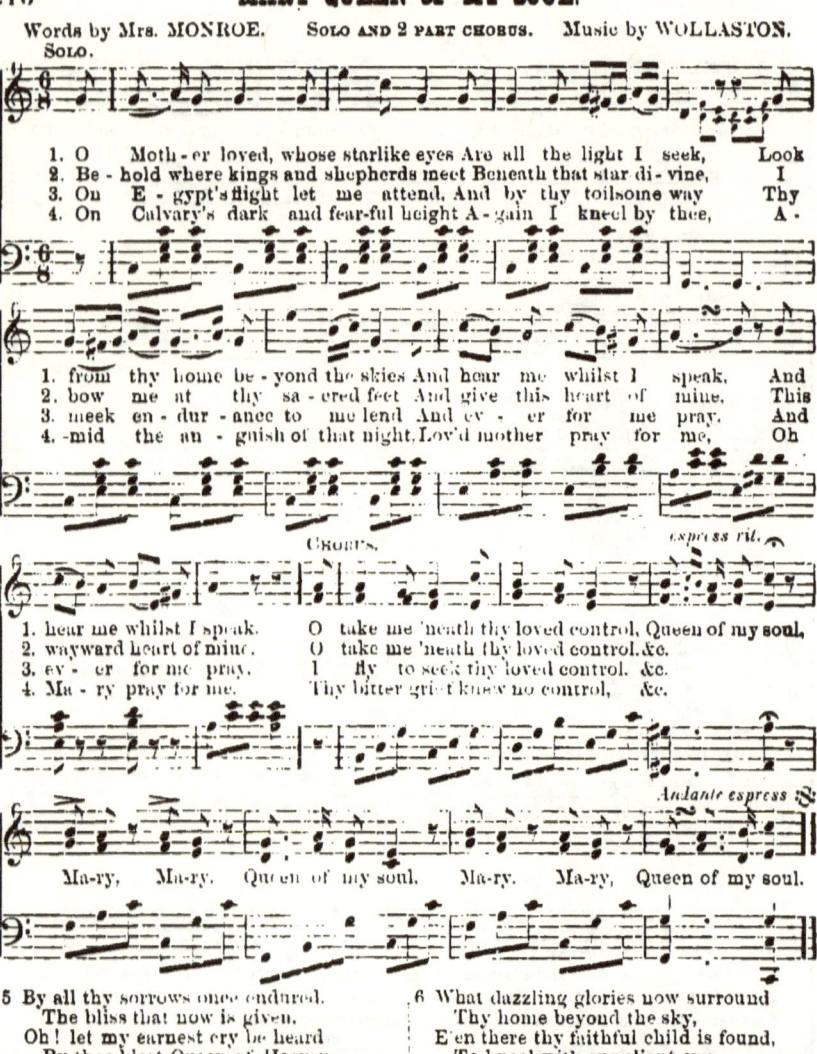

1. O Mother loved, whose starlike eyes Are all the light I seek, Look from thy home beyond the skies And hear me whilst I speak, And hear me whilst I speak.
2. Behold where kings and shepherds meet Beneath that star divine, I bow me at thy sacred feet And give this heart of mine, This wayward heart of mine.
3. On Egypt's flight let me attend, And by thy toilsome way Thy meek endurance to me lend And ever for me pray, And ev - er for me pray.
4. On Calvary's dark and fearful height Again I kneel by thee, A-mid the anguish of that night, Lov'd mother pray for me, Oh Ma-ry pray for me.

CHORUS.

O take me 'neath thy loved control, Queen of my soul,
O take me 'neath thy loved control, &c.
I fly to seek thy loved control. &c.
Thy bitter grief knew no control, &c.

Mary, Mary, Queen of my soul. Mary, Mary, Queen of my soul.

5 By all thy sorrows once endured,
  The bliss that now is given,
Oh! let my earnest cry be heard
  By thee blest Queen of Heaven.
  By thee blest Queen of Heaven.
CHO.—Bright angels bow to thy control,
  Queen of my soul,
  ||: Mary, Mary, Queen of my soul. :||

6 What dazzling glories now surround
  Thy home beyond the sky,
E'en there thy faithful child is found,
  To kneel with suppliant cry,
  To kneel with suppliant cry.
CHO.—Oh take me 'neath thy loved control,
  Queen of my soul,
  ||: Mary, Mary, Queen of my soul. :||

These Hymns are also published with Piano accompaniment, under the title of "May Chimes." Price, $1.25.

MARY'S TITLES.

(SOLO AND TWO PART CHORUS.)

Words by A. PROCTER. Music by S. N. D.

1. Thro' the world thy children raise Their pray'rs, and still we see, Calm are the nights and bright the days Of those who trust in thee.
2. Queen of heaven, when we are sad. Best so-lace of our pains. It tells us tho' on earth we toil, Our moth-er lives and reigns.
3. Hope of sin-ners, how ma-ny souls, Cast down by woe and sin, Have learn'd thro' this dear name of thine, A pardon and peace to win.
4. Ma-ry, dear-est name of all, The ho-liest and the best. The first low word that Je-sus lisped, Laid on his mother's breast.

CHORUS. *Animato, ad lib.*

Star of the sea, we kneel and pray, When tem-pests raise their voice, Star of the sea, the hav-en reached. We call thee, we call thee and re-joice, Star of the sea, Star of the sea.

HOLY MARY, MOTHER MILD.

HEART OF MARY.

DUET & TWO-PART CHORUS.

Andante Espressivo.   Peters' Sodality Book.

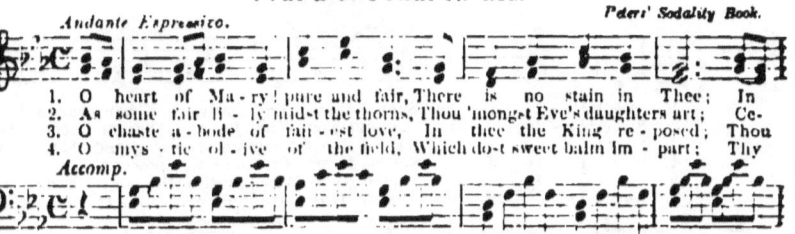

1. O heart of Ma-ry! pure and fair, There is no stain in Thee; In
2. As some fair li-ly midst the thorns, Thou 'mongst Eve's daughters art; Ce-
3. O chaste a-bode of fair-est love, In thee the King re-posed; Thou
4. O mys-tic ol-ive of the field, Which dost sweet balm im-part; Thy

Accomp.

CHORUS.

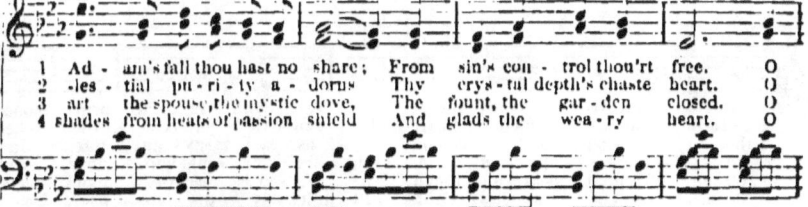

1. Ad- am's fall thou hast no share; From sin's con-trol thou'rt free. O
2. -les- tial pu-ri-ty a-dorns Thy crys-tal depth's chaste heart. O
3. art the spouse, the mystic dove, The fount, the gar-den closed. O
4. shades from heats of passion shield And glads the wea-ry heart. O

Heart of Mary! pure and fair, No beauty can with thine compare! From

ev-'ry stain of sin thou'rt free; O make us pure in heart like Thee.

5 As children to their mother flee
   When storm-clouds darkly lower,
   So loving hearts will haste to thee
     In sad affliction's hour.

6 As doves all innocent and pure
   Repose within their nest,
   So we from every ill secure
     In Mary's Heart shall rest.

7 Sweet Heart, within thy depths so chaste
   We'll dwell and ne'er depart,
   Till thou our souls hast deeply placed
     In Jesus' Sacred Heart.

8 And when from the loved heart we'll go,
   To that of thy dear Son,
   O shall we leave thee then — Ah no,
     His Heart and thine are one.

"Our Lady of Help." Concluded.

O SANCTISSIMA.

"Assumption." Concluded.

6 Lead me forever to adore
   The glorious One in Three;
   ||: And whilst I tremble more and more,
   O Mary! remember me. :||

7 Rose of the cross, thou thornless flower,
   May I thy follower be;
   ||: And when temptation wields its power,
   O Mary! remember me. :||

STABAT MATER.
SOLO and TRIO or THREE-PART CHORUS.

EVE OF MAY.

DUET OR 2 PART CHORUS AND SOLO.

Words by S. N. D.
Music by L. LAMBILLOTTE.

"Mary, Mother Sweet." Concluded.

O SANCTISSIMA.

SICILIAN.

JOY OF MY HEART.
MAY HYMN.
TRIO WITH BASS AD LIB.   LAMBILLOTTE.

1. Joy of my heart! O let me pay To thee thine own sweet
2. Thou, Mary, art my hope and life, The star-light of this
3. Thou who wert pure as driven snow, Make me as thou wert
4. Write on my heart's most secret core, The five dear wounds that

month of May; Mary, one gift I beg of thee,
earthly strife. Sweet Day-Star! let thy beauty be
here below; Oh! Queen of Heaven! obtain for me
Jesus bore, O give me tears to shed with thee,

My soul from sin and sorrow free, My soul from sin and sorrow free.
A light, to draw my soul to thee, A light to draw my soul to thee.
Thy glory there one day to see, Thy glory there one day to see.
Beneath the Cross on Calvary, Beneath the Cross on Calvary.

236. MARY QUEEN OF ALL THE FLOWERS.

Solo and Chorus.

Words by M. E. WALSH, Pupil of S. N. D.   Music by L. LAMBILLOTTE.

1. The bees are a-live in the clo-ver, Soft clouds are a-drift in the blue,...... The flow'rets their pe-tals un-cov-er, The blossoms are gleaming with dew...... Sweet Ma-don-na, the
2. The lil-y that dwelt by the wa-ter, Was breathing a song in the morn,...... A whisper of heaven it taught her, When first her young beauty was born...... Sweet Ma-don-na, low
3. The blossoms will glow for an hour...... In sunshine the bird-ling may sing,...... But fades the pale bud in the show-er. In win-ter the war-bler takes wing...... Sweet Ma-don-na, re-

MARY QUEEN OF ALL THE FLOWERS. Concluded.

1. ro - ses in their glad - ness Are shedding their fragrance a - new.... Smile
2. droop - ing, in her white - ness, Un - sul - lied by shad-ow or storm,... She
3. mem - ber when the snow-drifts Blow cold as the win-ter they bring, Our

1. on, there dwells no sad - ness, Where thou art gentle and true.
2. fain would seek thy bright - ness, Her fair - ness to a - dorn.
3. hearts know not De - cem - ber, For love is al - ways Spring.

CHORUS.

Queen of all the flow - ers, And La - dy of the spring. With-

-in thy own bright bowers, Thy ten - der - ness we sing....

HAIL, VIRGIN! DEAREST MARY! (May Hymn.)

CHORUS & SOLO.

Hail, Vir-gin! dearest Ma-ry, Our love-ly Queen of May, O spot-less, bless-ed La-dy! Thy chil-dren hum-bly bend-ing, A-round Thy shrine so dear, With heart and voice as-cend-ing, Sweet Ma-ry, hear our pray'r, Sweet Ma-ry, hear our pray'r.

Fine.

"Hail! Virgin, Dearest Mary." Concluded.

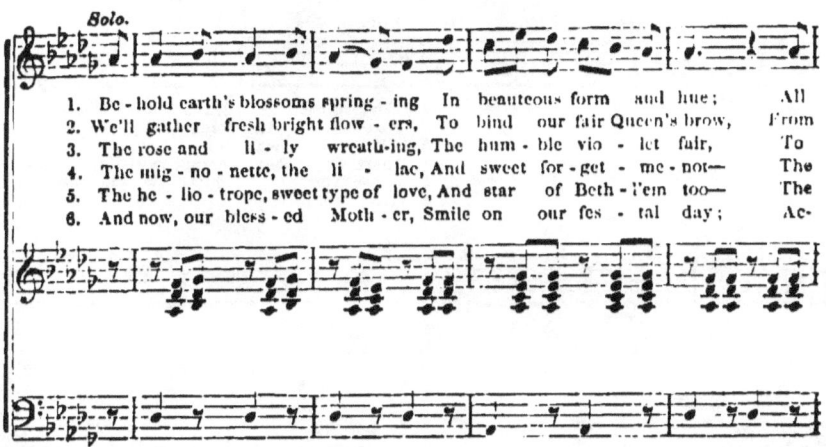

1. Be-hold earth's blossoms spring-ing In beauteous form and hue; All
2. We'll gather fresh bright flow-ers, To bind our fair Queen's brow, From
3. The rose and li-ly wreath-ing, The hum-ble vio-let fair, To
4. The mig-no-nette, the li-lac, And sweet for-get-me-not— The
5. The he-lio-trope, sweet type of love, And star of Beth-l'em too— The
6. And now, our bless-ed Moth-er, Smile on our fes-tal day; Ac-

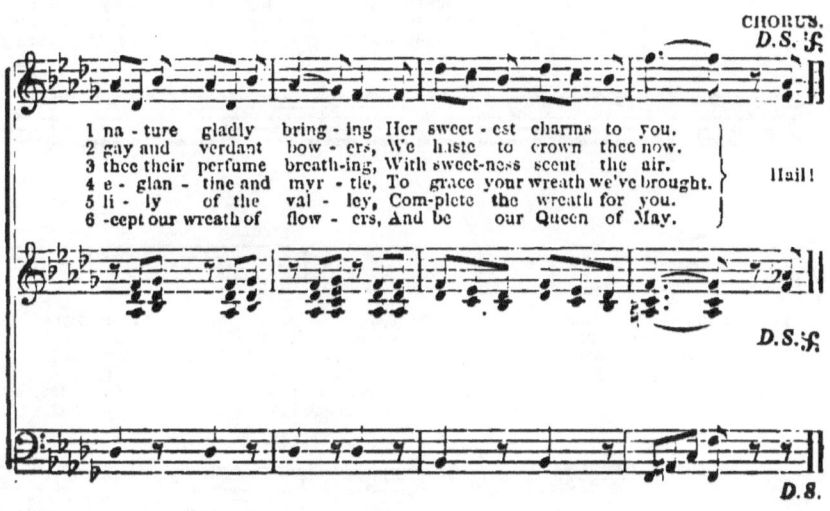

1 na-ture gladly bring-ing Her sweet-est charms to you.
2 gay and verdant bow-ers, We haste to crown thee now.
3 thee their perfume breath-ing, With sweet-ness scent the air.
4 e-glan-tine and myr-tle, To grace your wreath we've brought.
5 li-ly of the val-ley, Com-plete the wreath for you.
6 -cept our wreath of flow-ers, And be our Queen of May.

Hail!

"Farewell to May." Concluded.

HYMN FOR THE RELIGIOUS PROFESSION.

SOLO and TWO-PART CHORUS.

Words by S. N. D. *And. espress.* SOLO. Music by C. VON WEBER.

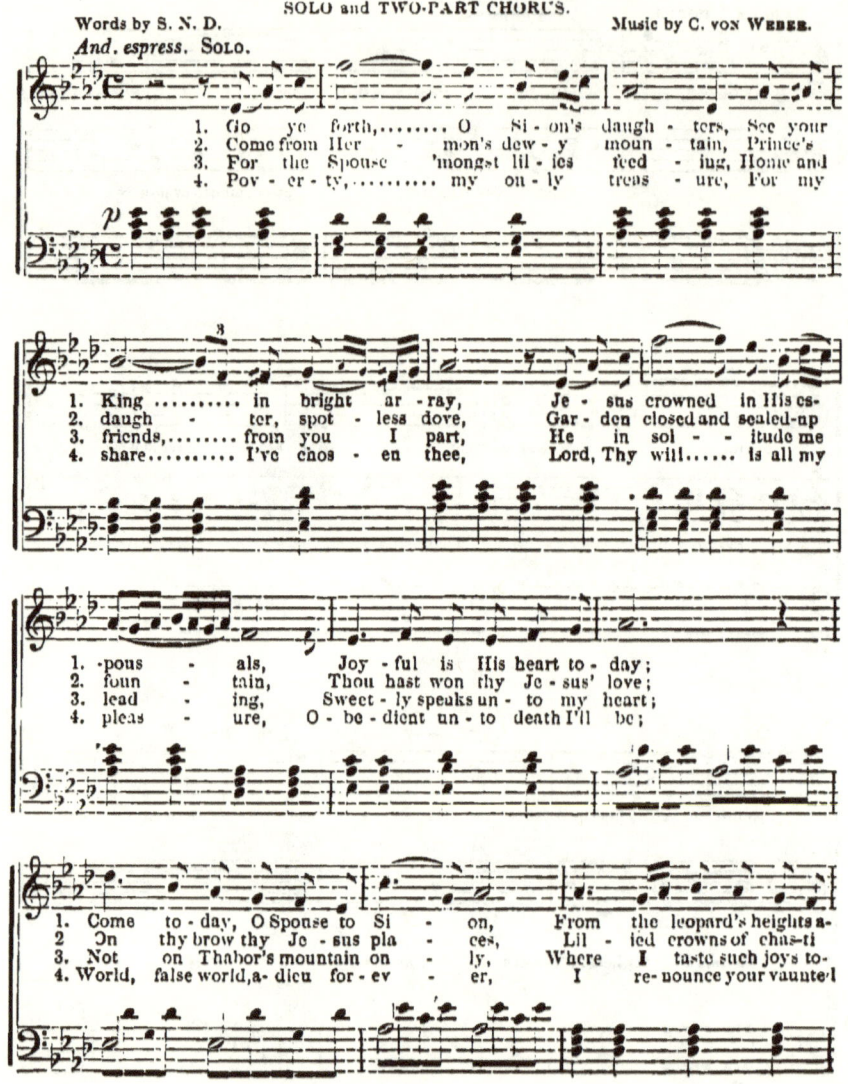

1. Go ye forth,......... O Si-on's daugh-ters, See your King......... in bright ar-ray, Je-sus crowned in His es-pous-als, Joy-ful is His heart to-day; 1. Come to-day, O Spouse to Si-on, From the leopard's heights a-

2. Come from Her-mon's dew-y moun-tain, Prince's daugh-ter, spot-less dove, Gar-den closed and sealed-up foun-tain, Thou hast won thy Je-sus' love; 2. On thy brow thy Je-sus pla-ces, Lil-ied crowns of chas-ti

3. For the Spouse 'mongst lil-ies feed-ing, Home and friends,......... from you I part, He in sol-i-tude me lead-ing, Sweet-ly speaks un-to my heart; 3. Not on Thabor's mountain on-ly, Where I taste such joys to-

4. Pov-er-ty,......... my on-ly treas-ure, For my share......... I've chos-en thee, Lord, Thy will......... is all my pleas-ure, O-be-dient un-to death I'll be; 4. World, false world, a-dieu for-ev-er, I re-nounce your vaunted

"Hymn for the religious profession." Concluded.

1. -round,...... From Li - ba - nus ...... and dens of li - ons,
2. -ty,......... He decks thy soul........ with price - less gra - ces,
3. -day,......... But on Cal - v'ry's sum - mit lone - ly,
4. charms,....... Earth and Hell........ com - bined can nev - er,

ritardo.   CHORUS. *con anima.*

1. Haste, to-day thou shalt be crowned.   I'm thine, my Je - sus, thine for-
2. Robes it with His pu - ri - ty.   I'm thine, &c.
3. With my Je - sus will I stay.   I'm thine, &c.
4. Tear me from my Je - sus' arms.   I'm thine, &c.

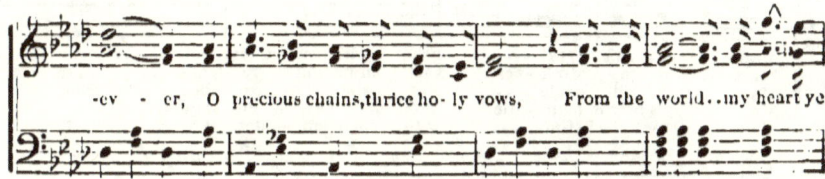

-ev - er, O precious chains, thrice ho - ly vows, From the world...my heart ye

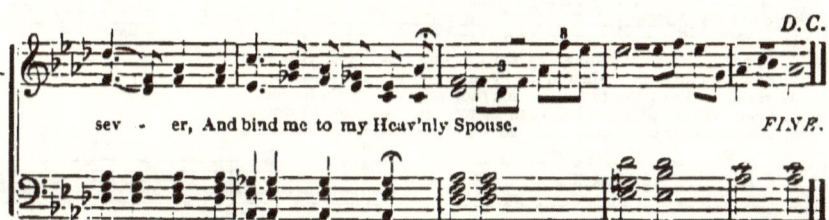

D.C.

sev - er, And bind me to my Heav'nly Spouse.   *FINE.*

HAIL! HOLY JOSEPH, HAIL!

5
Hail! holy Joseph, hail!
Teach us our flesh to tame;
And, Mary, keep the hearts
That love Saint Joseph's name.
          Hail, etc.

6
Mother of Jesus! bless,
And bless, ye saints on high,
All meek and simple souls
That to Saint Joseph cry.
          Hail, etc.

HYMN TO ST. PATRICK
DUET OR QUARTET.
Raphaelson.

"St. Aloysius." Concluded.

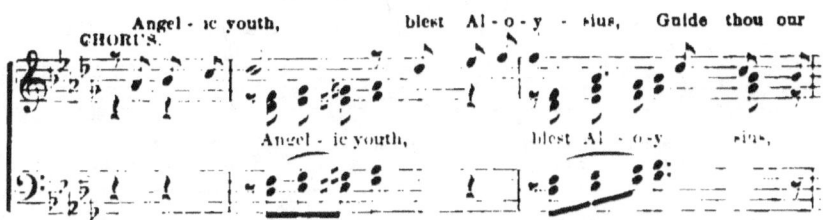

HYMN TO ST. AGNES.

DUET AND THREE-PART CHORUS.

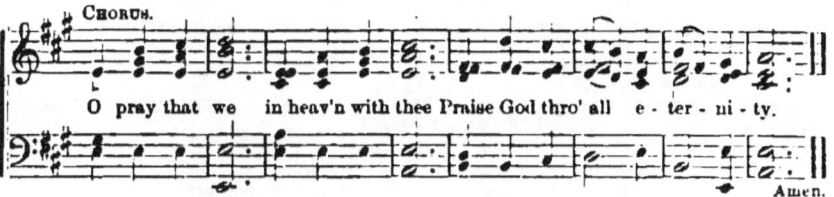

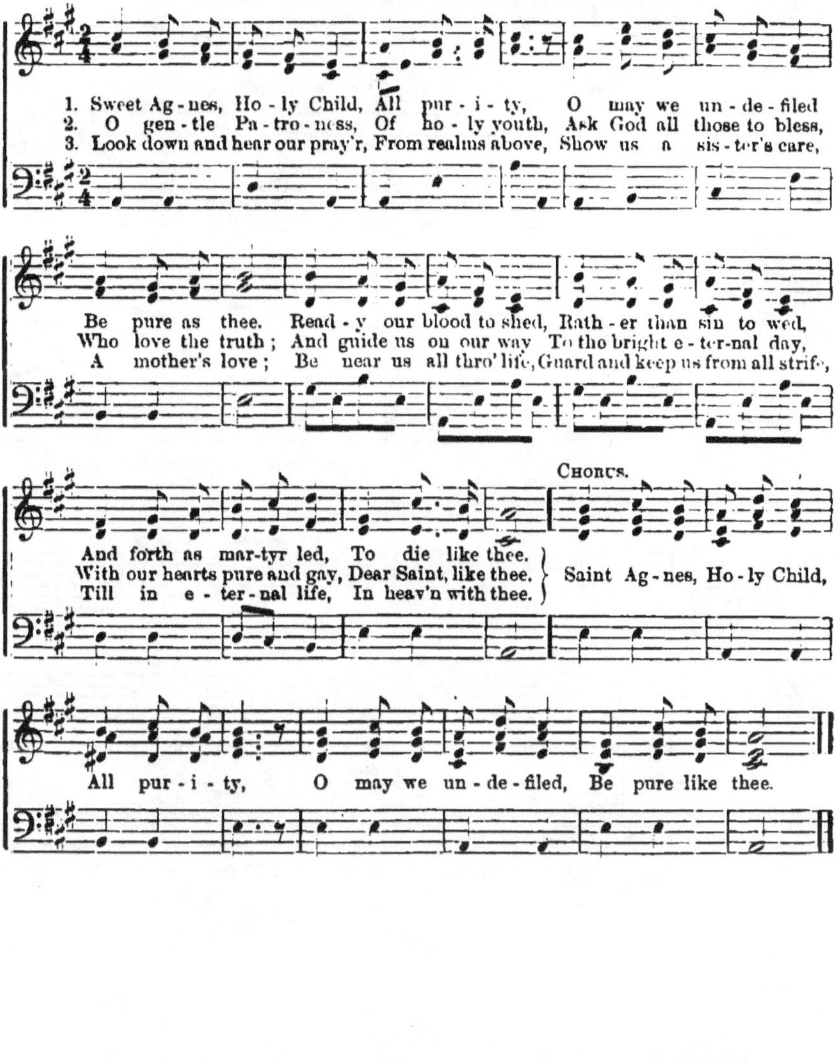

www.ingramcontent.com/pod-product-compliance
Lightning Source LLC
Chambersburg PA
CBHW021359230426
43666CB00006B/581